"Full disclosure—J.R. Briggs is an automatic read for me, and *The Art of Asking Better Questions* proves why. This book reignites the undervalued rabbinic skill of asking questions, showing how they can deepen relationships, strengthen leadership, and enrich faith. J.R. weaves together engaging stories, practical insights, and a genuine passion that invites readers to embrace curiosity as a way to connect more meaningfully with others and the world. After all, Jesus himself modeled this as the greatest question-asker of all time, and J.R. helps us follow in those footsteps. It's a compelling, thought-provoking guide for anyone who wants to live with greater intention, wonder, and discovery."

Leonard Sweet, author of *Decoding the Divine*, professor, preacher, publisher, and proprietor of Sanctuary Seaside advance center

"If a word aptly spoken is like apples of gold in settings of silver, then asking quality questions may be compared to a pearl of great price. If you would like to learn how to ask better questions and thereby cultivate a richer relationship with God and others, then why not give yourself the gift of this intriguing, insightful book by J.R. Briggs and make your world—and the world—a better place?"

Todd D. Still, Charles J. and Eleanor McLerran DeLancey Dean and William M. Hinson Professor of Christian Scriptures at the George W. Truett Seminary at Baylor University

"The invitation that this book offers us is breathtaking. Ask good questions. In a world of trite, algorithm-formed answers, the call of God's people is to learn to craft the best questions all over again. These questions are not new—they are simply new to us, which matters. Because when we look at Jesus, he didn't answer the bad questions. Because it's impossible to give a good answer to a bad question. We must return to the good questions. And J.R. Briggs has shown us how to do so."

A. J. Swoboda, associate professor of Bible and theology at Bushnell University and author of *A Teachable Spirit*

"Get ready to unearth some great treasures in J.R. Briggs's *The Art of Asking Better Questions* (and then record these gems to remember in what J.R. calls a Questions Journal). J.R. teaches the mindsets that allow for great questions (curiosity, courage, wisdom, and humility), and we learn powerful questions to deepen our relationships—in our spiritual lives, as leaders, or simply with people we want to befriend. I've already used J.R.'s questions for lament and spiritual growth in my own life. This book will inspire you and open up conversational pathways you've never imagined."

Heather Holleman, professor, speaker, and author of *The Six Conversations*

"If, as J.R. Briggs so powerfully communicates in the pages that follow, 'good questions are gifts we extend to others,' then reading this book feels like sitting next to the tree on Christmas morning. The quality of our lives truly is determined by the quality of questions we ask God, ourselves, and others, and this fantastic book helps you move toward better questions and a better life. What are you waiting for?"

Ben Malcolmson, motivational speaker and author of *Walk On: From Pee Wee Dropout to the NFL Sidelines*

"By far this is the best resource on becoming a person who asks great questions! The diverse research, helpful notes, numerous biblical examples, and tons of practical exercises make this a valuable book. I will be rereading, marking up, and sharing it with my tribe for years to come. J.R. Briggs's transparency is disarming, and his boldness is challenging—what a perfect combo! You've got to dive into this book, don't put it off—you won't regret it."

David Arthur, CEO and president of Precept and author of *Ordinary People, Extraordinary God*

"Who would have known that so much growth could come by asking better questions? Well, J.R. Briggs. This is something he's not just taught but also modeled for as long as I've known him. Many of us have been urging him to write this kind of book, and we are the better now that he has. Combining relevant research with inspiring stories and practical guidance, J.R. shows how our lives, relationships, and world might be enriched by asking better questions. I hope it will be read by leaders, teachers, and every person who wants to grow."

Keas Keasler, associate professor of spiritual theology at Friends University

"J.R. Briggs has written a timely and important book. The questions we ask determine the kind of life we live. J.R.'s skillful, pastoral, and practical analysis of the power of questions in our lives is a gift to us all. Hoping God uses this book so we can ask better questions and live more fruitful, missional, and God-honoring lives."

Jon Tyson, author and pastor of Church of the City New York

"What if the key to deeper leadership isn't having the right answers but asking better questions? This book is a powerful reminder that questions expand perspective, deepen engagement, and strengthen connections. In today's ever-changing world, few skills are more vital for leaders. With this conviction, J.R. Briggs provides a road map for cultivating curiosity by offering examples, practical frameworks, and a treasure trove of hard-hitting questions. If you want to live and lead with greater depth, humility, and impact, *The Art of Asking Better Questions* is an essential guide."

Shannon Kiser, senior director of Fresh Expressions North America

"In *The Art of Asking Better Questions*, author and 'professional question-asker' J.R. Briggs challenges readers to reflect on these information-eliciting expressions that compose so much of our language: questions. More than attracting information, attending to questions cultivates curiosity, enhances awareness, and places a renewed and sharpened focus on the world outside us—persons, places, and things. Using entertaining illustrations and accessible writing, J.R. invites readers to see questions not merely as instruments of information but as a means of formation."

Kevin Brown, president of Asbury University

"The world is filled with too many answers that are facile, manipulative, or shallow. But a good question opens the door to self-awareness, healthy relationships, and spiritual depth. J.R. Briggs invites us to follow the way of Jesus, who used good questions to dignify and dive in, to clarify and confront, to reframe and renew. And he shows us how to do the same."

Gregory L. Jao, senior assistant to the president and director of diversity and external relations for InterVarsity Christian Fellowship/USA

"In an age dominated by simple answers, J.R. Briggs demonstrates the power of curiosity and engaged inquiry. J.R. shows how good questions do more than reveal information or direction; they bring us into relationship with God and others who challenge, encourage, and shape our thinking and encourage our souls. Life is better because of questions, and J.R. will guide you in the art of cultivating questions for transformation."

Michael Hammond, president of Gordon College

"J.R. Briggs asks the best questions of anyone I know. This book inspires both humility and curiosity—often missing in us—to see and seek to understand the other. It has already made me more intentional about how I ask questions."

Alex Cameron, Anglican bishop of Pittsburgh

"There is nothing less interesting than an answer without a question. Yet all too often, Christians are guilty of rushing to offer answers rather than patiently asking questions and listening to the questions that are on the hearts and minds of our neighbors. I know of no better guide for becoming a better question-asker than J.R. Briggs. Having been on the receiving end of J.R.'s thoughtful questions, I have experienced the rare gift of being truly, deeply listened to. I highly recommend this to anyone, especially leaders."

D. J. Marotta, priest and author of *Liturgy in the Wilderness* and *Our Church Speaks*

"J.R. Briggs is a master teacher of the art of asking better questions. To open these pages is truly to open yourself to a world of becoming a better person. Read this book and experience some of the greatest questions ever asked and, in return, some of the truest encounters with people ever recorded. In these most antagonistic of times, this is what we need: Christians who can ask better questions and can encounter people as persons."

David Fitch, B. R. Lindner Chair of Evangelical Theology at Northern Seminary

"When it comes to living a whole and healthy life, one of my favorite teachers is J.R. Briggs. If you've been feeling a disconnect in your leadership, community, or relationships, here is a book that will breathe new life into tired systems. In *The Art of Asking Better Questions*, J.R. not only teaches us why questions are so important, but he shows us how to ask them with nuance, sensitivity, and love."

Emily P. Freeman, author of *How to Walk into a Room*

"I can't remember the last time that I read a book that caused me to stop mid-sentence and try something new in real time. But J.R. Briggs's book *The Art of Asking Better Questions* has become both an inspiration and a goad. Like all good art that doesn't come easy, the desire to ask better questions has been frustrating for me. But through this book, I have been inspired to become a more artful questioner and have shared with my entire consulting team lessons from the book that are making all of us better."

Tod Bolsinger, founder of AE Sloan Leadership and author of *Canoeing the Mountains* and the Practicing Change Series

"I didn't even need to finish the first chapter before I had a handful of insights I could apply immediately to my work. The best leaders ask the best questions, but most of us have never been taught how. My only wish is that I'd have read this book sooner."

Tim Schurrer, author of *The Secret Society of Success* and CEO of David Novak Leadership

"'What is my favorite mistake and what did I learn from it?' J.R. Briggs has once again provided a thought-provoking and practical approach to living and loving all aspects of our lives with each other. My regret is that I did not ask myself this transformative question years ago! Query and fear not! J.R. is here to provide you with no answers!"

Robert Wonderling, former president and CEO of the Philadelphia Chamber of Commerce

THE ART OF ASKING BETTER QUESTIONS

Pursuing Stronger Relationships, Healthier Leadership, and Deeper Faith

J.R. BRIGGS

ivp

An imprint of InterVarsity Press
Downers Grove, Illinois

InterVarsity Press
P.O. Box 1400 | Downers Grove, IL 60515-1426
ivpress.com | email@ivpress.com

InterVarsity Press® is the publishing division of InterVarsity Christian Fellowship/USA®. For more information, visit intervarsity.org.

All Scripture quotations, unless otherwise indicated, are taken from The Holy Bible, New International Version®, NIV®. Copyright © 1973, 1978, 1984, 2011 by Biblica, Inc.™ Used by permission of Zondervan. All rights reserved worldwide. www.zondervan.com. The "NIV" and "New International Version" are trademarks registered in the United States Patent and Trademark Office by Biblica, Inc.™

While any stories in this book are true, some names and identifying information may have been changed to protect the privacy of individuals.

The publisher cannot verify the accuracy or functionality of website URLs used in this book beyond the date of publication.

Cover design: Faceout Studio, Spencer Fuller
Interior design: Jeanna Wiggins
Cover image: © oxygen / Moment via Getty Images

ISBN 978-1-5140-1111-9 (print) | ISBN 978-1-5140-1112-6 (digital)

Printed in the United States of America ♾

Library of Congress Cataloging-in-Publication Data
Names: Briggs, J. R., 1979- author
Title: The art of asking better questions : pursuing stronger relationships, healthier leadership, and
    deeper faith / J.R. Briggs.
Description: Downers Grove, IL : InterVarsity Press, [2025] | Includes bibliographical references.
Identifiers: LCCN 2025011297 (print) | LCCN 2025011298 (ebook) | ISBN 9781514011119 paperback |
    ISBN 9781514011126 ebook
Subjects: LCSH: Spiritual life–Christianity | Inquiry-based learning | Interpersonal relations–Religious
    aspects–Christianity
Classification: LCC BV4501.3 .B75227 2025 (print) | LCC BV4501.3 (ebook) | DDC 248.4–dc23/
    eng/20250623
LC record available at https://lccn.loc.gov/2025011297
LC ebook record available at https://lccn.loc.gov/2025011298

32   31   30   29   28   27   26 | 12   11   10   9   8   7   6   5   4

To my father, Dave Briggs,

who has embraced the power and significance

of asking great questions and continues

to live the question-oriented life.

I am better because of it—and so are many others.

The quality of your life is determined by
the quality of the questions you ask
God, yourself, and others.

The one who asks questions does not lose his way.

AFRICAN PROVERB

CONTENTS

PART 1

TOO MANY ANSWERS

What makes a good question?

What's the difference between a good question and a truly great one?

What is it about the power of a question?

Why do some questions grip us and refuse to let go?

Why are we often quick to give answers but slow to ask questions? Is it that we don't know how or that we don't find them all that important?

Are we confident in our answers but insecure in our questions?

Are we too impatient? Or uninformed? Or uninterested?

Are we afraid of what we might find out or where it might lead us?

Have we become too enamored with answers?

Introduction

WHY DO WE ASK QUESTIONS?

Without a good question, a good answer has no place to go.

CLAYTON CHRISTENSEN

We are exploring together. We are cultivating a garden together,
backs to the sun. The question is a hoe in our hands and
we are digging beneath the hard and crusty
surface to the rich humus of our lives.

PARKER PALMER

WE LIVE IN A WORLD that has conditioned us toward answers. We've been taught to give the right answers, yet little attention has been given to teaching us how to ask the right questions. We don't have a shortage of information; we have a shortage of wisdom, curiosity, and wonder. Asking good questions is a lost art.

What if our obsession with the right answers is blinding us to the power of better questions? What if we learned to ask the right questions at the right time for the right reason?

When he was a boy, Albert Einstein asked himself, "What would you see if you were traveling on a beam of light?" This question led to the theory of relativity.

In his presidential inaugural address in 1961 on the steps of the US Capitol, President John F. Kennedy stated, "Ask not what your country can do for you, but what you can do for your country." This shift in questions cast a vision for what a unified and others-oriented nation could look like.

In the 1980 US presidential election, Jimmy Carter's campaign slogan was, "A tested and trustworthy team." Ronald Reagan's was, "Are you better off than you were four years ago?" Reagan won by a landslide.

The sixteenth-century Spanish saint Teresa of Avila wrote, "When one reaches the highest degree of human maturity, one has only one question left: *How can I be helpful?*" Her writings continue to be read and revered.

Dr. Martin Luther King Jr. stated, "Life's most persistent and urgent question is, *'What are you doing for others?'*" His vision continues to help us wrestle with the issue of race in America.

Have you ever noticed that America's national anthem, "The Star-Spangled Banner," penned by Francis Scott Key in 1814, is nothing more than two long questions?

Have you ever paid much attention to the questions you ask? And have you considered why you ask questions at all?

The questions we ask often reveal the values we hold.

The questions we ask determine the life we live.

Consider the most significant questions you've asked or been asked in your life.

Who am I?

What will I do with my life?

What's most important to me?

What is true, good, and beautiful?

Will you follow me?

Will you accept the job?

Will you trust me?

Will you marry me?

I'm a professional question-asker. As a faith-oriented leadership development coach and consultant, I'm called to ask questions of leaders from a wide variety of backgrounds and vocations every day. I've read dozens of books on asking questions. Over the years I've studied and interviewed countless leaders and their questions. I've written various articles on the topic. I've taught at numerous training events and facilitated a wide variety of trainings around it. I wrote my dissertation on how to equip faith leaders to ask better questions for deeper impact. I've been thinking deeply and ironing out the concepts around this topic for well over a decade. In many ways, it feels like I've been working on this book my entire adult life. But before I wrote this book, I was convinced I had to live it first; it had to be written inside of me.

I'm passionate about questions because I have seen the impact they can have in people's lives—and in my own. The more I study, utilize, and train people around questions, the more convinced I become: questions are a powerful force in the world, far more potent than we've given them credit for. And yet, I've not arrived; I never will. I'm still learning how to ask questions of substance and significance. None of us fully arrives, but we can all improve in the questions we ask.

I have a bone-deep conviction that all of us need to ask more questions—and *better* questions. Doing so can change your life and the lives of those around you. I'm not the only one who is convinced that questions are powerful. Dozens of research studies have revealed their numerous benefits. People who ask frequent questions are more popular among their peers and more often seen as leaders. They have more social influence and are sought out more frequently for friendship and advice. Asking better questions helps you to navigate crucial conversations effectively and handle conflict productively. And they lead to more effective reading comprehension.

They also have massive neurological effects. Questions stimulate your brain, releasing serotonin and a rush of dopamine. They trigger a reflex called instinctive elaboration, which takes over your thought process, rendering you incapable of thinking of anything else. Questions are so powerful researchers have described them as having the ability to hijack our brains. Let me give you an example: What color are the shoes you're wearing? (See what just happened—you couldn't help it, could you?) Our thoughts are shaped by the questions we're asked. While most of us believe we're good at multitasking, numerous studies reveal that humans are terrible at it. Which means that when you ask someone a question, you have *hijacked their thoughts*, even if for just a brief moment. A good question is an invitation for participation and engagement—with others and inside your own body.

To be clear, this is not a book of 1,001 best questions to ask at your next dinner party (although I've taken the liberty to italicize some thoughtful questions throughout as well as list some of my favorite questions in the back of the book). Nor is this book a formulaic, follow-these-seven-steps-add-water-and-stir approach. As the title suggests, asking great questions is an art. Nobody should create a spreadsheet and declare they are 37.4 percent better at asking today than they were last quarter. Asking better questions is a mindset. It is a posture. A way of life. Growing in our asking is not about ticking off a checklist of dos and don'ts. There is no paint by numbers kit included in this book.

Instead, I want to travel upstream to help you take a closer look at the questions we ask—or refrain from asking. *Why are questions, with all their potential and power, so grossly underutilized? What are the forces that keep us from asking questions? And how can we learn to ask better ones?* I want to help raise the value and priority of questions, increase your desire to inquire, and help raise your Question/Answer ratio. Because when you raise your Q/A ratio and improve the quality of your questions, everyone wins—*everyone.*

This book includes scores of suggestions for how to improve what you ask. But let me warn you: if you set out to implement all of them at once, you'll quickly become overwhelmed. I want to suggest a different approach: read with a pen or highlighter in hand. When you come across an idea you find interesting and might like to try, underline it, circle it, or write yourself a note in the margins. Then when you've finished the book, revisit your markings and pick a few practices to start with. (And, if you prefer, a few blank pages are in the back for you to write your own notes or thoughts.)

I'll lay all my cards down on the table here: this book is not for everyone. If you're content with the current status of your relationships, the quality of your conversations, and the way you think about life, faith, and the world, let me encourage you: put this book down before you go any further. Your time will be better spent on other things. This book is for people who want to go deeper—with God, friends, family members, coworkers, colleagues, and neighbors—and even with themselves.

The irony is not lost on me that this is a book about question-asking—and here I am offering statements about questions. Friends have ribbed me throughout the writing process, asking me if this book would be written entirely with questions. Thankfully, for both your sake and mine, it is not. Certainly, answers play an important role in the world. We need answers. If I am going into surgery, the last thing I want is a surgeon asking the nurses what they think should be done. Answers provide information, perspective, and crucial context to how we think, feel, and act. And yet, it astounds me how much power can be found in asking questions and how easily accessible that power is to every one of us. Questions are free and readily available, yet they remain largely untapped. Now is the time to awaken the sleeping giants from their latent state and unleash their power for good in the world.

DIFFERENTIATING BETWEEN QUESTION-ASKING AND QUESTIONING

It's important to differentiate between *questioning* and *question-asking*. Questioning someone or something can be helpful at times, but it can often assume a posture of distrust, confrontation, or doubt. When we feel we are being questioned, we may go on the defensive and feel uncomfortable and suspicious. Or when people question the faith of others or their own, it can sometimes lead to conflict, division, and doubt. Whether fairly or unfairly, people who ask these types of questions are often labeled as revolutionaries, doubters, cynics, rebels, troublemakers—even heretics.

But this questioning posture is not what this book is about. Instead, this book is primarily about *questioning-asking,* where we seek to ask questions that emphasize honor, care, discovery, and growth. It encourages wonder, or what we might call holy curiosity. It's more about possibility than doubt, more about creativity than cynicism. These kinds of questioners ask, *"Can you tell me more about . . . ?," "I wonder if . . . ?,"* and *"Imagine if we considered . . . ?"* These questions hold the power to unlock the doors of discovery and place us on the path toward new paradigms, creative solutions, and previously unimagined ideas.

WHAT ARE GOOD QUESTIONS LIKE?

Good questions are gifts we extend to others.

They are like keys on a key ring, capable of unlocking doors and opening new passageways.

They are windows by which we see others and mirrors by which we see ourselves.

They are archaeologists' tools—trowels, shovels, and spades—excavating hidden treasures lying beneath the surface.

Good questions are flashlights shining a light on where we need to go next.

They are screwdrivers that pop open a stuck lid on a can of paint.

They are like neck muscles that move the head to focus on certain things and turn away from others.

And some questions are like gadflies and midwives. They are tools used to leverage good in the world, but we don't use the same tool in every situation. Therefore, we need wisdom to discern which tool to use when.

Asking great questions has the power and potential to improve the quality of every single area of life—your relationships, your career, your faith, and your future. It can have a significant impact on neighborhoods, schools, churches, workplaces, and online. In fact, *there's not a single area where improving the quality of the questions you ask won't improve the quality of your life and the lives of those around you.* Few things can bring about change more effectively than the right question. Once you see how rich and textured and colorful the world can be with better questions, you won't want to turn back.

EXPANDING—OR SHRINKING—YOUR WORLD

The dimensions of your life expand or shrink in proportion to the questions you ask.

I remember the first time I asked two significant questions. Little did I realize how those two questions would change the trajectory of how I would approach potential opportunities throughout my life. I was a junior in college studying abroad at a school perched atop Mount Zion in Jerusalem in the fall of 1999. Our class was on a three-day field trip journeying through northern Israel and the Galilee region. Before dinner one evening, I went for a stroll along the eastern shore of the Sea of Galilee and noticed a commercial fishing boat arriving at a dock nearby. Since I was a kid, I'd wanted to go fishing on the Sea of Galilee with commercial fishermen, the guys who did this for a living day in and day out, to get a better understanding of some of the important stories in the Gospels. As I saw these fishermen, my heart raced with an idea. But then reality set in. I started thinking of all the reasons why they would say no. *I shouldn't ask. It's silly. It'd be a waste of time.*

But then two questions popped into my head. *What's the worst they could say to me? Can I handle a no?* Yes, the worst someone might say to me would be "no." Or maybe "Absolutely not, you're crazy." Or a mocking laugh followed by a "Get out of here!" I thought further. *So what if they do? I'll never see them again. I can handle getting turned down. So I guess it makes sense for me to go ahead and ask . . .*

With nothing to lose, I sauntered over to the crew and asked if I could speak to the captain of the ship. A man with a wizened face, leathery skin, and a stern look stepped forward and said his name was Menachem. "For most of my life I've wanted to go fishing on the Sea of Galilee," I said. "Can I go out with you and your crew tomorrow on your boat? Put me to work all day—and for free. Actually, I will pay you fifty dollars if I can join you."

In a thick Jewish accent and with no emotion, Menachem said, "I don't need your money. Just meet us here at 6 a.m. tomorrow and you can come." Then he turned and walked back to the boat to unload the day's catch with his crew. I stood there stunned. A lifelong dream was about to happen. I was in. The next day's adventure on the lake was one of the most memorable experiences from my entire semester in Israel. Memories of that time on the water remain seared in my mind to this day. And all I did was ask.

Those two questions—*What's the worst they can say? Can I handle it?*—have opened numerous doors and ushered in new opportunities I never would have imagined. Later that semester I spent the night with a Bedouin family sleeping soundly in their tent and eating the most incredible Middle Eastern cuisine. A few weeks later, I assisted Palestinian shepherds in the birth of a baby lamb in the Judean wilderness. A few years later I served as an AAA minor league baseball mascot for three seasons. I had my tuition fees covered for my master's degree when I proposed a creative idea to the president. For twelve years I was mentored by Eugene Peterson up until he passed away. I've been a balloon handler in a Thanksgiving Day Parade. I've been able to interact with many people I've admired and respected. I say all this not to brag but to emphasize the immense power and possibility of asking good questions. In each of these situations, people have asked me,

"How in the world did you get the chance to do that?" and my answer is always the same: "I just asked." These two simple questions have shifted my outlook from *Why?* to *Why not?*

Undoubtedly, I've also received countless rejections, but in those moments I knew I could handle them. I still had to ask. But let me be clear: there have been times when I thought about asking but didn't. Why? Because I couldn't pass the test of the second question. There have been times when I was emotionally wobbly and insecure, or when I didn't want to jeopardize a relationship by running the risk of making things unbearably awkward. But what has surprised me most is how often people have not only said yes but have also said yes quickly and gladly. I still ask these two questions frequently. Because when you refrain from asking questions your world shrinks, but when you start to ask better questions more frequently your world starts to expand.

BECOMING AN ILLUMINATOR

Why do some people seem to be better at asking questions than others? Are great question-askers made or born? I sense it's both. But I'm convinced that everyone can learn to ask better questions if they have a desire to grow and a commitment to learn. Certainly, some professions require the skill and proficiency to ask great questions. Reporters, journalists, attorneys, physicians, philosophers, therapists, hostage negotiators, and *Jeopardy!* contestants come to mind. So do competent mechanics, consultants, teachers, leadership coaches, and talk show hosts.

But you don't need an advanced degree to improve your questions. You don't have to host focus groups for an ad agency, become a therapist, or work for Gallup. Asking great questions isn't reserved solely for a courtroom, an interrogation room, or an NPR studio. They can be utilized effectively every day in the classroom, the boardroom, the living room, and the playroom. Regardless of your vocation, location, stage, or status, you can grow to ask questions of substance and significance.

David Brooks wrote a profoundly personal and invaluable book titled *How to Know a Person*. His chapter "The Good Questions" is worth the price of the book itself. In it he writes,

> In every crowd there are Diminishers and there are Illuminators. Diminishers make people feel small and unseen. They see other people as things to be used, not as persons to be befriended. They stereotype and ignore. They are so involved with themselves that other people are just not on their radar screen. Illuminators, on the other hand, have a persistent curiosity about other people. They have been trained or have trained themselves in the craft of understanding others. They know what to look for and how to ask the right questions at the right time. They shine the brightness of their care on people and make them feel bigger, deeper, respected, lit up.

This book was written with that central purpose in mind: to help you become a better Illuminator by your questions.

What if you left behind stale conversations and stepped into more meaningful connections?

What if the way you connected with others was not through power, control, and performance but through humility, engagement, and trust?

What if you weren't seen by others primarily as intelligent or authoritative but as curious, caring, and wise?

What if?

WHY OUR APPROACH TO QUESTIONS NEEDS TO CHANGE

What keeps us from asking questions?

It is easier to judge the mind of a man by his
questions rather than by his answers.

PIERRE-MARC-GASTON DE LÉVIS

Once you have learned how to ask questions—
relevant and appropriate and substantial questions—
you have learned how to learn and no one can keep you
from learning whatever you want or need to know.

NEIL POSTMAN AND CHARLES WEINGARTNER

DARYL DAVIS HAS ONE OF the most unique collections you'll ever come across: he owns more than two hundred Ku Klux Klan (KKK) robes and hoods. What makes his collection even more unique is that Davis is African American.

An accomplished jazz and blues musician, he has met with and befriended countless members of the KKK over the past thirty years. Many of them had never met or interacted with a Black man until they met Daryl. Through Davis's proactive and compassionate pursuit of friendship, he's helped many leave the Klan altogether. Each robe and hood he owns was given to him as a gift by each of his new friends when they decided to leave the group for good. His dream is to open a museum one day and put them on public display.

What spawns these unlikely friendships? During his first meeting with a Klansman, Davis asks numerous questions and listens patiently. But there's one he always utilizes: "Why do you hate me when you know nothing about me?" That simple yet piercing question greases the skids for deeper understanding—and helps add more robes to his collection. *What if a question is nothing more than an invitation to think?*

But if questions are so forceful, capable of changing even the perspectives and convictions of scores of KKK members to leave for good, why don't we ask more of them? Questions, it seems, aren't very sexy. At times, they can imply weakness, ignorance, insecurity, even disrespect or rebellion. They can easily be misunderstood. They can seem inefficient—an interruption, distraction, or detour from the task at hand.

In our world, which elevates accomplishing tasks over deepening relationships, it makes sense that questions aren't held in high esteem. We value pragmatism, individualism, and efficiency. Certainly, there are times we need to tell to be helpful. But if we're honest with ourselves, sometimes we just want to win an argument or gain control of a situation, conversation, or person. Other times we want to portray our intelligence. Telling is often much more efficient, and our brains like certainty.

With the omnipresence of smartphones and the immense growth of artificial intelligence, the availability of information is, quite literally, at our fingertips. And with the advancement of modern technology, we don't even need our fingers now. With a quick voice command, we're capable of retrieving information faster and more easily than at any time in human history. The deck seems to be stacked against questions. And yet, *if we are looking for better answers, should we not start by asking better questions?*

WHAT IS THE PURPOSE OF A QUESTION?

What is a question? In its simplest form, it is communication that desires a response. It is the salt of communication, seasoning everyday conversations and interactions. Without salt, the food of our conversation would provide sustenance, but it would create a bland and largely transactional—and forgettable—experience. Think about how different the world would be if language was composed only of declarative statements, commands, and assertions. There would be no way to engage with another person other than to talk *at* them. Heather Holleman, professor at Penn State University and author of *The Six Conversations,* has spent years researching and speaking about what happens when we connect with others in a conversation and the common barriers that keep us from connecting. When I asked her what a question's purpose is, she offered these two clear responses: *clarity* and *engagement.*

Stories play a central role in our lives. They shape how we see the world and ourselves. Philosopher Alasdair MacIntyre, in his book *After Virtue,* wrote, "I can only answer the question, 'What am I to do?' if I can answer the prior question 'Of what story or stories do I find myself a part?'" Questions remind us that we are in a story and that we have a part to play in it.

Recently, I was heating up some leftovers for lunch in the microwave at my coworking space. I saw a colleague I hadn't talked to in a while sitting at the table eating by himself. I was tempted to say, "What's up?" or "How ya doing?" but decided to be a bit more intentional.

"Hey, Trevor. What's giving you joy these days?" I asked.

Normally he's a light and warm guy, but he seemed heavyhearted, his gaze downcast.

"Not much actually. I've just lost two family members in the past month. It's been hard to find joy lately . . . ya know?"

I sat down, expressed my sympathy, and asked him a bit more. He said attending these two funerals back to back was difficult, but he admitted he'd been asking questions he normally wouldn't be asking himself. *Who am I really? What am I doing with my life, and is it making a difference? Have I told my family often enough that I love them?* Funerals have a way of forcing us to ask ourselves what story we are a part of. *Clarity.*

And questions are tools for engagement. Questions help us to lean in further, move conversations forward, and cultivate deeper relationships. Questions are a significant weight-bearing beam in each one of our meaningful relationships. Asking questions also has significant implications on romantic relationships. Maybe you've heard of the research by psychologists Arthur and Elaine Aron, who wanted to see if strangers could create close bonds simply by asking a list of thirty-six questions. Some of them included *What would constitute a perfect day for you? For what in your life do you feel most grateful? When did you last cry in front of another person?* The Arons' research was popularized by a *New York Times* article by Mandy Len Catron, who went on to marry the man who participated in the experiment with her. No, it's not a surefire way to find a partner or spouse, but the Arons were on to something important. The process of asking the right kinds of questions led to cultivating connection and intimacy.

Rhetorical questions are also about engagement. They are catalysts of recalibration, forcing us to rethink our ways. They scrutinize our presuppositions and help to dismantle assumptions (and we know what assumptions can do to you and me). Oftentimes the question *is* the answer. *Wouldn't you agree?* For a time, printers used a backward question mark at the end of a sentence to indicate a rhetorical question, but the practice eventually died out in the seventeenth century. Personally, I'd love to see that practice restored. When we're asked a rhetorical question, we're forced to wrestle with a preinstalled follow-up question: *How would I respond to that? Engagement.*

CHILDREN AND QUESTIONS

As every parent knows, children are natural question-askers. They are hardwired with an innate sense of curiosity and an insatiable desire to learn. They are experts at imagination and play, which is often prompted and sustained by questions. They feel uninhibited to ask about anything because everything is new. They, quite literally, have fresh eyes; they are the underappreciated research and development department of the human race.

The average child asks roughly forty thousand questions between the ages of two and five. During this three-year span, a shift occurs in the kinds of questions the child asks. By two and a half, they shift from asking questions about simple facts to ones that require more complex explanations. By their fourth birthday, the lion's share of the questions demonstrates a hunger for explanations, not just facts. A recent study revealed that the average four-year-old girl in the UK asked her mother 290 questions in a typical day. Yet sadly, by middle school these children had almost completely ceased asking questions. When we enter regular schooling age, the desire to inquire wanes significantly.

So what happens to children in the years between preschool and middle school? Many teachers and learning experts lament that our current educational system doesn't encourage inquiry-based learning. In some cases, questions aren't even tolerated. The primary educational emphasis in most public schools is to teach students how to sit quietly and retain information passively. *Repeat after me. Memorize the information. Regurgitate on the test.* As our sense of permission and comfort in asking questions goes down, so does our desire to ask them.

For years children take courses in math, history, and science, but how many of us have ever taken a course on how to ask questions or become active listeners? I know a few people who hold degrees in journalism and law who tell me they have, but outside of these particular fields, it's rare. We've been taught what to think, but it's much more difficult to find a school that teaches how to think about question formation. Our current model of test taking always reveals aptitude when requiring students to adequately provide answers to questions on the exam. Have you ever taken a test where the answers were provided for you and your grade was based primarily on the quantity and quality of thoughtful questions you generated from those answers? Yeah, you're not alone. While many teachers have appreciated questions in the classroom for a long time, almost all questions and answers have occurred between teachers and students. Seldom is permission given to encourage learning by having students ask questions of each other. *Why is this?*

Author Neil Postman, an early and vocal critic of the traditional educational approach, wrote, "Is it not curious, then, that the most significant intellectual skill available to human beings is not taught in school? I can't resist repeating that: The most significant intellectual skill available to human beings is not taught in school." Postman also stated, "This is why students enter school as questions and leave as periods." They become experts in giving answers and novices at asking questions. Similar to Postman, Rabbi Abraham Joshua Heschel wrote that in our society, the priority should not be on the evaluation of students' answers but on the formulation of the questions they are able to generate themselves. One could rephrase the ancient Chinese proverb to say, "Ask students a question and they inquire for a day; teach students how to ask questions and they will inquire for a lifetime."

The words *educator* and *education* come from the word *educe*, which means to draw or bring out something latent; to cause to appear, to elicit. *What if teaching was less about giving students new information and more about awakening what is already inside of them? What if it really is about educing?*

I'm not casting aspersions on well-meaning and hardworking teachers. I, too, am an educator. I regularly speak to groups of people, preach sermons, teach courses, and give lectures at various colleges and seminaries. But oftentimes our educational system, driven by standardized test scores, discourages even our best and most curious teachers from taking this approach. I know it's not all educational institutions, but I'm convinced: we can do better. The best teachers I've ever had—whether in an academic setting or in the classroom of life— were those who asked great questions. A seminary professor frequently asked our class, "How will this information help you to love God and love your neighbor more fully?" Years ago, a mentor looked at me and asked, "What's most important to you?" Years ago, my youth pastor asked a roomful of students, "How will you make your life count for someone beyond yourself?" Those questions have remained with me. When they had a choice between asking a question that was informative or incisive, they often chose the latter.

Not all educational approaches are built on passive consumption. The classical school and Montessori educational approaches have eschewed traditional educational frameworks, embracing instead a self-directed, student-focused model. Well-known graduates of Montessori education include former food television personality Julia Child, Google cofounders Sergey Brin and Larry Page, and Amazon founder Jeff Bezos, among others. Bezos believes so strongly in this educational approach that he pledged $2 billion through his Day One Fund toward Montessori schools in underserved communities.

It is impossible to acquire effective *thinking* skills unless we first possess effective *questioning* skills. For founder Maria Montessori, it all began with a few foundational questions: Why are we sending our kids to school in the first place? What if our schools could train students to be better lifelong learners and better adapters to change by enabling them to be better questioners? And thus, how might we create such a school? Similarly, leaders at the Right Question Institute sought to do just that. They developed the Question Formulation Technique, encouraging just one change to the educational approach:

instead of teachers asking all the questions to their students, train the teachers to push their students to ask them. "The world is so complicated," stated Nancy Cantor, former chancellor at Syracuse University, "the best thing we can do for students is to have them ask the right questions."

OBSTACLES THAT KEEP US FROM ASKING QUESTIONS

Why, then, don't we ask more questions? In my research I've discovered eight obstacles.

Obstacle one: We live in an attention-seeking age.

"Enough about me," the adage goes, "what about you? What do *you* think about me?" We live in a culture that is defined by the tireless pursuit of attention and self-absorption, and thus, we don't often think about asking questions. It just doesn't cross our minds to ask. We are tempted and sometimes even expected to compete for attention at work, in social functions, and online. We seek to suck in as much attention and approval as we can, much like an asthmatic gasping for oxygen. When we're thinking about ourselves, we hardly have any space or energy to think about others. Boston College sociologist Charles Derber calls this conversational narcissism. *How will people pay attention to what I am doing if I don't point the conversation toward me? How will I get people to notice me if I ask thoughtful questions of them?*

Young basketball fans grow up dreaming of becoming like Michael Jordan or LeBron James. Jordan was my favorite player growing up. But nobody dreams of becoming John Stockton. In fact, many may have never even heard of him. Standing at just over six feet tall and weighing 170 pounds, he was small and unimpressive by National Basketball Association (NBA) standards. (It didn't help that he wore some of the shortest shorts the league had ever seen.) Yet he finished his NBA career as a ten-time all-star and helped lead the Utah Jazz to the playoffs in each of his nineteen seasons. He played on the 1992 gold-medal-winning US Olympic team (dubbed the "Dream Team"), was named one of the fifty greatest players in NBA history, and was inducted into the Hall of Fame. Most impressive, though, he still holds the NBA records for most career assists and steals—by eye-popping margins. We live in a "shoot first" age that wants to talk and give answers. Asking questions is a "pass first" mentality. Shooting first may make you better, but learning to be a great passer makes the entire team better. In a world of Jordans and LeBrons, it's not cool to be a Stockton. What if we helped to change that?

Obstacle two: We think we know already.

Warren Berger, author of two wonderfully helpful books on questions and a self-described questionologist, believes that one of the biggest barriers is knowledge. We don't ask because we think we already know enough. It seems counterintuitive, doesn't it? The more you know, the less you feel the need to ask. It's called the trap of expertise, and it's easy to fall into it. *If I'm already convinced that I know the answer, why ask at all?*

We can become so sure about how the world works that we never pause and ask, *How do I know for sure?* Ray Dalio, founder of Bridgewater Associates, the world's largest hedge fund, experienced a seismic failure in his early life that he now credits as the reason for his later financial success. In that failure, he shifted from thinking, "I'm right," to asking himself, "How do I know I'm right?" That shift changed the course of his life. The more close-minded we are, the fewer questions we'll ask. Of course, we must always be mindful of our blind spots and biases. But what makes them so frustrating is that, inherent to their definition, we can't see them. The truth is we don't know as much as we think we do. Living a question-oriented life helps to keep us grounded in the reality that there are things we don't know we don't know.

Obstacle three: It's perceived as inefficient and unhelpful.

Questions are often seen as unproductive. In our fast-paced, efficient, productivity-oriented world, it feels as though someone has slammed on the brakes of progress when they ask a question. We favor task accomplishment over relational depth. Leaders often feel the need to act decisively and quickly and can become anxious about the perceived inefficiencies that questions might bring. Questions often force us to slow down and think. In our fast-paced world, who has much time for that?

In 1970, American futurist Alvin Toffler wrote, "The illiterate of the twenty-first century will not be those who cannot read and write, but those who cannot learn, unlearn, and relearn." Many of the most important questions help us to unlearn old patterns and assumptions and require us to relearn. Growth and discovery are hardly efficient. In a world that values—even worships—efficiency, questions can feel frustratingly intrusive and annoying. *Forget questions,* we might think, *we just need answers.* But are they the answers we need?

Obstacle four: It isn't modeled well.

More is caught than taught. We struggle to know how to be a good father if we grew up in a home without one. We can't master the new software being installed across all of our systems at work if we don't receive proper training. Unfortunately, many of us spend a significant amount of time in places and situations where thoughtful question-asking is discouraged and even punished. We are often conditioned to stick to what we've learned: either give smart answers or keep our mouth shut. Sometimes it's in our family systems or schools. Other times it's in local churches or social settings. These places are called question deserts. *If we aren't in environments where questions can be asked freely and openly, how and where will we learn how to do it?* If we are surrounded by people who continually give answers and few, if any, are asking good questions, we tend to think that this is just the way it is. *How can we know how to do something well if we haven't seen it modeled well? How can we learn something if no one has explicitly taught us how to do it?*

Obstacle five: We don't care to know what other people think.

Let's be honest: sometimes we just don't care to know the answers people might offer when we ask a question. It could be because of apathy, exhaustion, arrogance, or a lack of curiosity. Author and coach Michael Bungay Stanier writes that we love to give advice to others— we *love* it. But if we can build the simple but difficult habit of taming what he calls our Advice Monster, we can stay curious a little longer and not rush to give advice. Asking curious questions is one of the greatest ways we can tame the Advice Monster when it begins to rear its ugly head. Unfortunately, a lack of curiosity can become a breeding ground for stereotyping, rigid thinking, dogmatism, and even discrimination, as we learned in Daryl Davis's experiences with the KKK. When it becomes extreme, it can lead to hatred and violence.

Obstacle six: We're afraid of awkward interactions or what we might learn.

Questions can be risky. Asking good questions is a vulnerable act. It's a verbal admission that you don't know something. Our environment discourages asking questions in a thousand little ways. What if we don't know the answer and we look incompetent in front of others? What if people misunderstand our question and perceive us as being uncooperative or disagreeable—or worse, arrogant and disrespectful? We might ask a good first question, but what if we don't know what to say or ask next?

David Brooks noted that our world is insecure and self-protective, which equates to a world with fewer questions. In many corporate settings, leaders have had questions beaten out of them years prior, often because they learned the hard way. Asking questions can even be hazardous to one's career: raising one's hand in the conference room and asking a question is to risk being seen as uninformed, insubordinate, or both. Sometimes the only way to survive is to give intelligent answers rather than offer questions. There are often unspoken rules and expectations when it comes to leadership across cultures. In some cultural contexts it may be more hierarchical or deferential, as asking questions of elders or those in authority can be perceived as disrespectful or offensive.

Obstacle seven: *We assume people don't want to be asked.*

We erroneously assume people always want to be left alone. Sure, we all need our time away from people—some more than others—but the truth is many people are deeply lonely and long to be known. Most people want to be asked about their lives to share what matters most to them. The late Chicago journalist Studs Terkel was known for collecting oral histories. He found great joy in asking others deeply thoughtful questions, then sitting back and just listening. He said, "Listen, listen, listen, listen, and if you do, people will talk. They always talk. Why? Because no one has ever listened to them before in all their lives. Perhaps they've not ever even listened to themselves."

Obstacle eight: *It can be hard work and requires deliberate practice.*

Even if we've been given permission to ask questions and it's been modeled well, it doesn't mean it's easy. Neurologist John Kounios observed that the brain is always seeking ways to reduce our mental workload, and one of those ways is to simply accept things without question—or to even ignore much of what is going on around us at any given moment. We often operate on autopilot. While crafting good questions comes naturally to children, we grow out of it as adults. Few of us have developed a specific plan with actionable practices to increase the quality of our question-asking. A paltry number of employees has participated in official training to receive the proper tools and develop the necessary skills to ask great questions. *What if every organization offered formal training for their employees to ask better questions?*

BUT IS IT WORTH THE EFFORT?

Sometimes we fail to ask questions not because we don't care but because we don't have the energy. Many of us go through the day feeling mentally, emotionally, and physically depleted. Several months ago on a flight from Philadelphia to Dallas, I saw a middle-aged woman wearing a T-shirt that read, "Too tired to care." Sometimes we just don't possess the relational bandwidth, physical capacity, or mental willpower to ask questions. We may think, *Where will I find the time to learn to ask better questions? Do I have the energy to overcome these obstacles?* There's both bad news and good news here: Yes, asking new and better questions is extra work. It may make our brains hurt at times. But it is worth it. The payoff is incredible.

Nothing is as simple and complex for us as learning to ask great questions. Growing in our question-asking skills may seem as daunting as walking barefoot across hot coals. Despite the obstacles and the time, energy, and attention needed to grow in it, there's good news: it's not insurmountable. Asking better questions is as much about attitude as it is aptitude. You may feel it's too hard to master—let alone learn—the art of asking better questions. But you can do it. It's worth the effort to learn. The world, and your world, will be better because of it.

THE POWER AND POSSIBILITY OF QUESTIONS

Why do we ask questions at all?

*The minute we begin to think we have
all the answers, we forget the questions.*

MADELEINE L'ENGLE

*Always the beautiful answer who asks
a more beautiful question.*

E. E. CUMMINGS

PARKER PALMER HAD BEEN OFFERED the position of college president, and he was ready to accept. He had already visited the campus, talked with the board, faculty, and administration, and was told the job was his if he wanted it. Because he was a Quaker, he gathered about a dozen friends for a clearness committee, a communal practice of discernment his religious tradition holds when someone is at the crossroads of a significant decision. In a clearness committee, friends sit with their discerning companion for three hours—not offering answers or dispensing advice but simply asking questions, believing that the questions will help clarify what is most important. Palmer admitted later his true motive in gathering his friends together was not discernment but to have an opportunity to brag about being offered the job, one he was determined to accept.

His friends' first few questions were easy, and he answered them quickly and sufficiently. About halfway through, one friend asked what seemed to be another easy question—at least on the surface. But it was much more difficult than he imagined: "What would you like most about being president?"

He paused a full minute before offering a reply. "Well, I would not like having to give up my writing and my teaching. . . . I would not like the politics of the presidency, never knowing who your real friends are. . . . I would not like having to glad-hand people I do not respect simply because they have money. . . . I would not like—"

At that point, a friend gently yet firmly interrupted to remind him that was not the question at hand: What would you *like* about being president? Parker offered an answer that came from his deepest parts, one that appalled him even as he said it.

"Well, I guess what I'd like most is getting my picture in the paper with the word *president* under it." His answer was laughable; his friends knew it, and so did he. But the group knew something of great significance was at stake, something greater than a job offer. The answer remained in the air. After a few moments, someone asked a question that cracked everyone up and cracked Palmer open: "Parker, can you think of an easier way to get your picture in the paper?"

Parker later reflected, "By then it was obvious, even to me, that my desire to be president had much more to do with my ego than with the ecology of my life—so obvious that when the clearness committee ended, I called the school and withdrew my name from consideration. Had I taken that job, it would have been very bad for me and a disaster for the school." One seemingly simple question—and then a follow-up—changed the trajectory of Palmer's vocational life.

WHAT DO QUESTIONS DO?

Consider the power and potential of questions in various fields.

Problem solving. Leaders who seek to solve problems, or generate new ideas and solutions, ask two main questions: *What is?* and *What if?* Research by Mihaly Csikszentmihalyi found that Nobel laureates were far better at achieving breakthroughs once they found the right question to reframe their problem.

The Maltese physician Edward de Bono is most known for his work with lateral thinking, whereby he developed the concept of the six thinking hats. The process helps groups think by wearing different colored "hats." He found the mind thinks in several different modes and methods, which can be utilized through questions. When facing a problem, groups can engage in a deliberate process:

The white hat: What information are we missing, and how can we get it? (facts)

The red hat: What are our fears or concerns overall about this project? (gut feelings)

The black hat: What are the downsides and risks to this idea or project? Why wouldn't this work? (pessimistic thinking)

The yellow hat: What are the benefits we would gain from this? (optimistic thinking)

The green hat: What other options might exist? What else? (alternative and additional options)

The blue hat: Which hat do we need to wear and when in the process? What else should we consider that we've not yet done? (a big picture focus on the process itself)

Over the years, I've used de Bono's process numerous times with different groups and teams—and in almost every instance, we've arrived at new insights and clearer thinking that ultimately led to confident decision-making.

Innovation and idea generation. Steve Jobs was a proponent of the principle known as *shoshin*, or "beginner's mind." With a beginner's mind there are many possibilities, but with the expert's mind there are only a few. It's akin to adopting a mindset called neoteny, the phenomenon of maintaining childlike mental attributes as an adult. Asking purposefully naive questions—even seemingly unintelligent ones—tends to be a gift, not a liability. Kevin Kelly, technologist, author, and cofounder of *Wired Magazine*, wrote, "A good question will be the sign of an educated mind. A good question is one that generates many other good questions. A good question may be the last job a machine will learn to do. A good question is what humans are for."

What's more, entrepreneur and author Keith Ferrazzi noted, "If you ask questions that are like no other, you get results that are unlike any that the world has seen. How many people have the courage to ask those questions? The answer: all the people responsible for the great innovations." All great innovation and creative ideas were preceded by a question that sounds something like, "What if we . . . ?"

Business. Just a few years after he cofounded Apple in a garage in Northern California, Steve Jobs sought out John Sculley to become the company's new leader. This was no easy request, as Sculley was CEO of PepsiCo, which at the time was a massive $2 billion food and beverage corporation. Jobs would be asking one of the most successful businessmen in the world to take a huge step down as well as a significant pay cut. Unsurprisingly, Sculley declined the offer. But over the years the two became friends, and Jobs would occasionally make the same bold offer.

One afternoon, when the two of them were sitting on a balcony overlooking New York's Central Park, Jobs turned to Sculley and asked, "Do you want to sell sugar water for the rest of your life, or do you want to come with me and change the world?" Sculley finally agreed. When a question is posed like that, how does one turn down *that* offer? At its fundamental level, isn't business ultimately about listening, making offers, and asking questions?

Executive Scott Gilbey learned how to sell not from a sales rep but by observing a purchasing manager named Ron.

"What's your best price?"

"$590,000."

"Is that your best price?"

"Okay, $570,000."

"Is that your best price?"

"Ron, you're killing me. Will $530,000 get me the order?"

"Is that your best price?"

"My boss is going to fire me. We will have no margin left. $520,000."

Ron never got emotional, argumentative, or manipulative. Never once did Ron say, "Your price is too high," nor did he suggest the vendor lower the price. He just asked the same question repeatedly. What is selling? It's an ask. Everyone is selling something. So what are you selling?

Troubleshooting. Taiichi Ohno, the mastermind behind the Toyota Production System, helped develop an effective brainstorming exercise called the "Five Whys," which helps teams address difficult issues. The concept is simple: for every complex problem, the team would ask why five consecutive times. For example:

Question 1: *Why did this project go past schedule?* It was much more complex than our team imagined.

Question 2: *Why was it more complex than our team imagined?* We had to start over in designing the product several times.

Question 3: *Why did we have to start over in designing the product several times?* The product was more difficult to use than we realized and confused our customers.

Question 4: *Why was the product more difficult to use than we realized and confused our customers?* We assumed our customers held the same understanding and expertise of the product as our engineers.

Question 5: *Why did we assume our customers held the same understanding and expertise of the product as our engineers?* Because we didn't test our product with market research as thoroughly as we should have, nor did we truly listen to the needs of our customers.

Bingo.

This can also be a valuable exercise in our everyday lives. I've engaged in this exercise various times—and it works. It's amazing what happens when you drill down to the real issue or problem. When you need to get to the root of a difficult issue, just ask why five times.

Journalism and media. Of all the fields where question-asking is essential, journalism and media may be the most obvious. Investigative reporters and talk show hosts, local reporters and beat writers, and even Oprah Winfrey and Malcolm Gladwell need to ask questions. The ability to arrive at the right answers depends in large part on the quality of the questions being asked. These skilled artisans of inquiry instinctively understand the power of a great question. It's amazing what happens when you skillfully and intentionally utilize the fundamental tools of who, what, where, why, when, and how.

Education. A mind with no questions is a mind not yet intellectually alive. Every academic sector and field of study exists only to the extent that new questions are generated and continue to drive thinking forward.

Steve Jobs reportedly ended meetings at Apple by asking two questions: "What's the thing I made most confusing?" and "What's the thing you learned in here that will most help you out there?" I found these to be so helpful that I used them in the seminary courses I taught in practical theology. I always reserved the last few minutes of each class to leave space for these questions. Oftentimes I found that my students' most significant learning occurred during those final few minutes. Think how different the academic experience is when the dominant question is "What can I learn that will help me better understand this subject and how it might prepare me for my future?" instead of "What do I need to do to get a passing grade in this class?"

Relationships. The pleasure people feel after talking about themselves activates the same areas of our brain as do money, sex, and choc-
olate. Researchers conducted a series of studies where people could
decide to either get paid to answer trivial questions about others or
answer questions about themselves for free. Interestingly, people enjoyed talking about themselves so much that they chose to disregard
about 20 percent of the money they could have earned. In another
study, researchers found that when people were getting to know one
another, those who asked more questions were better liked—and the
people who asked follow-up questions were liked even more. Simply
put, people like people who ask them questions.

Three mornings a week, I swim at my local YMCA. A few years ago,
during one of the breaks between my sets, a frail octogenarian I'd never
seen before was in the lane next to me.

"Young man," he said, getting my attention.

"Yessir."

"Wanna race?" he asked with a smile and a wink.

It was a small relational touchpoint, but one I still relish. I'd never
seen him before that interaction and I've not seen him at the pool since,
yet I've thought about that interaction countless times over the past
few years. I may have won the race, but he won the day.

Faith. As humans, we see the world through a unique set of lenses:
our worldview. We all have one. Each of our worldviews is shaped by
the answers we provide to a set of important questions. I write as a fol-
lower of Jesus rooted in a Christian worldview shaped by the answers
to several essential questions of life: *What is real? What is true? What
is good? What does it mean to be human? Where do I derive ultimate
purpose and meaning? What is our destiny?* We'll explore this connection between faith and questions a bit later in the book.

I find it both interesting and significant that the first question in the
Hebrew Scriptures was not asked by God or humans but by Satan in
the form of a serpent. The question was equally devastating and

devious: "Did God really say, 'You must not eat from any tree in the garden?'" (Gen 3:1). It was this rhetorical question that eventually led to the fall of the human race. Satan, the father of lies, knows exactly what questions to ask and how to ask them. He even knows when we are most susceptible to the lies implanted within those questions. He knows how to use questions to undermine and create doubt in our minds and hearts about God and his character and about our worth and identity. *Why would God continue to love someone like you? Is God really going to continue to be faithful to you and your family after all the times you sinned against him? Who do you think you are?* A lie is often communicated more compellingly not as an answer but as a question.

THE SECRET SAUCE

Asking good questions isn't limited to just the fields we covered. A few years ago, I was invited by the owner of a barber academy to lead a half-day seminar on how to ask good questions for their barbers in training. I shared about my experience with my barber, Tom, who owned his own shop. He gave decent haircuts, slightly above average. The wait times to get a haircut at his place were inconveniently unpredictable and often long. Though I had many different options of where to get my hair cut within walking distance of my house, I kept returning for only one reason: Tom always asked me great questions, ones that truly made me think. They were genuine, interesting, and thought-provoking questions that always led to meaningful conversations. *What do you appreciate most about being a dad? If someone gave you a free ticket to fly anywhere in the world for a week, where would you go and why? What book have you been reading lately that you've thoroughly enjoyed?* We would swap stories and laugh together. I looked forward to my time in the chair each month, and I think Tom enjoyed our times together too.

One summer, Tom went on a monthlong family vacation overseas and closed the shop while he was away. In need of a haircut that couldn't wait, I booked a time with another barber shop close to my house.

There was no wait time, and the haircut was great. In fact, it was one of the best haircuts I'd ever received. On top of that, it was less expensive than what Tom charged. But the next time I needed a cut, I went right back to Tom's place—and every month after that until he retired and sold the shop.

"Why didn't I return to the shop that gave me a great cut?" I asked the barbers at the training event. "Because that barber never asked me a single question during our time together." In fact, when I asked him questions, he offered uninspiring one-word responses. He seemed like he was either bored or inconvenienced. To me, receiving an average haircut while being asked great questions was more valuable than receiving a great haircut from someone else who asked average questions—or no questions at all. One was a connection, the other a transaction. If you think about it, there are few places in our world today where you literally just sit and do nothing. You don't read a book, scroll on your phone, or sleep. You just sit. Few, if any, situations are better suited for genuine question-asking and rich conversation than with a barber or stylist.

During that training event at the barber academy, I told them, "You are receiving top-notch training from some of the best barbers in the area, and soon you will be more than capable of giving great cuts. But pure skill isn't going to be enough to retain customers. However, if you can cultivate the skill of asking good questions of each client who sits in your chair, you'll create a deep bond that will keep your schedules full, and you'll develop customers for life." At this point, they were hooked. We spent the rest of the morning engaged in exploring and discussing how and what to ask clients during cuts.

A few months later, my family was out for dinner at our favorite Mexican restaurant when two young men approached our table. They introduced themselves and said they recognized me from the barber academy training. One told me, "Asking thoughtful questions matters. People keep booking with me because we're creating relational bonds in the chair. My calendar is always full now. Questions truly are the secret sauce." If it can benefit barbers, it can benefit you too, no matter what field you may be in.

BETTER QUESTIONS, BETTER ANSWERS

Here's a universal principle about questions: if you ask unthoughtful and unintentional questions, you'll almost always receive forgettable and bland answers—but if you ask genuine and intentional questions, you'll most often receive thoughtful and meaningful answers. Author and podcast host Krista Tippett writes, "Questions elicit answers in their likeness. Answers mirror the questions they rise, or fall, to meet. . . . It's hard to meet a simplistic question with anything but a simplistic answer."

Want generic answers? Ask generic questions. It's as predictable as a communist election.

But if you want more thoughtful responses, ask thoughtful questions instead.

Ask and you shall receive.

QUESTIONS TO ASK TO MAKE CONVERSATIONS GO DEEPER AND LAST LONGER

When did you realize . . . ?
How did you feel when . . . ?
What did you learn from . . . ?
Who helped you to . . . ?
Why did you/didn't you . . . ?
How are you different now because . . . ?
Why does it bring you immense joy to . . . ?

Asking a friend or acquaintance "How are you?" at a social event is fine and culturally acceptable. But leaning in with a bit more intention and asking, "What's been the highlight of your week so far?" or "What two or three adjectives might you use to describe how your family is doing in this season?" brings out much more interesting conversation. Asking a candidate in a job interview "What is your greatest strength?" won't help you very much in assessing their qualifications and fit for your organization. But ask, "What skill or personality trait do you possess that few people know you have that could be utilized in a work environment?" and you'll learn much more about them. As Tippett says, "It's hard to resist a generous question. We all have it in us to formulate questions that invite honesty, dignity, and revelation. There is something redemptive and life-giving about asking a better question."

THE FOUR ESSENTIALS TO ASKING GREAT QUESTIONS

What, then, is required of us if we want to ask great questions? There are four core essentials: curiosity, wisdom, humility, and courage.

Curiosity. English political philosopher Thomas Hobbes argued that science, religion, and even language exist because of the exploration of questions. Throughout his lifetime, Albert Einstein perceived curiosity as something holy, stating, "I have no special talents. I am only passionately curious." Curiosity shines a spotlight, brings awareness to our assumptions and blind spots, and opens doors.

I love the way the Cambridge Dictionary defines the word: "an eager wish to learn about something." Though it's easy to assume that curiosity just happens to us, it doesn't—we have to choose it. It's a skill, a muscle we develop, and it's essential to asking questions and ultimately to growth. Plain and simple, you cannot grow without curiosity. It is impossible to be curious and judgmental at the same time. So much division and polarization happen when we refuse to choose a posture of curiosity. We jump to conclusions. We assume things about others. When things are different, it's easy for our minds to think it's weird or even wrong. But press pause for a minute. What if instead we first stepped back and asked ourselves, *Is different bad, or is it just different? Can I see this from a different perspective right now? I wonder why this is the way this is.*

Rabbi Abraham Joshua Heschel wrote, "I did not ask for success; I asked for wonder." Curiosity and wonder are the seeds that sprout into great questions. We must have what David Brooks calls an active curiosity, an explorer's heart. Curiosity might kill cats, but it jump-starts relationships, generates new ideas, and paves the way for intimacy and connection in humans.

Wisdom. As we grow in our curiosity and our awareness of the power of questions, we must wield that power wisely. Questions can be beneficial or damaging, purely altruistic or diabolically unethical. They can bless and honor or shame and embarrass. They can be self-serving or others-focused. The questions we ask, how we ask them, and why we ask them at all reveal a great deal about who we are at our very core. Two of the most revealing differences between wise and foolish people are how they act and the questions they ask or refrain from asking.

Because of the significant power and potential of questions, wisdom is essential. Simply asking any question in any situation is not the right approach. In fact, asking the wrong question at the wrong time can lead to some cringeworthy moments, deep confusion, and even hurt feelings. But it's a beautiful thing when the right question is asked at the right time in the right situation—and with the right motive. In the first century, Jesus told his followers to be as shrewd as snakes and as innocent as doves (Mt 10:16). This certainly applies to questions. We need to double major in snakes and doves by seeking to be culturally sensitive and aware as we ask.

Humility. Curiosity grows from a deep-seated belief that what you don't know is more interesting that what you already know. This requires intellectual humility. It does not matter how brilliant you think you are; if you're not curious, you will be incapable of asking great questions. When you're in a place of unknowing, you are in a perfect position to learn with humility.

Great question-askers are fully aware of and quite comfortable with their ignorance. Curiosity is the driving force behind a good question. To be curious is to humbly admit that you don't know something and that you long to learn more. Richard Wurman, founder of the widely recognized TED conferences, liked to boast, "I know more about my ignorance than you know about yours." The best posture in asking questions is to assume you don't yet know the answer—and to consider other people to be better than yourself and to look to the interests of others, something the apostle Paul instructed us to embody (Phil 2:3-4). The most fundamental question might be, *Do you have sufficient self-esteem to be humble when you ask questions?* That's intellectual humility.

We live in a world full of mystery, which means there are some questions we'll ask that will never be fully answered. This is a good thing. But here's the truth: almost always, there is someone somewhere who knows the answers—and an important key to life is having enough humility to learn to ask the right questions of the right people. And this always involves a certain level of risk.

Courage. Curiosity requires us to be confident in our lack of knowing, to willfully admit we are ignorant about a particular topic. Because questions pack such a forceful punch, they demand stalwart conviction. Maybe you've been in a group setting where you didn't fully understand what was being discussed and thought, *I'm confused and I need some clarification here, but I don't want to ask a question because I might sound stupid.* Me too.

To ask a question is to run the risk of looking unintelligent or unprepared. To inquire is to have the ability to think clearly about what you don't know—or at least, what you don't know yet. We can be wise, curious, and humble, but if we don't have a little bit of courage, the chances are low that we'll ask at all. We need to possess the appropriate balance of confidence and humility to ask the questions that few people, if any, are currently asking.

THE LIMITS OF QUESTIONS

Questions may be the secret sauce, but they do have their limits. As the author of Ecclesiastes wrote, "There is a time for everything" (Eccles 3:1-8). By this we can confidently understand that there are times for asking questions and times to refrain from asking them. We've all been in situations where too many questions were asked, and it was unhelpful, unsettling, and maybe even irritating.

Because of my love of questions, I often assume people love them as much as I do. A few years ago, while waiting at the gate for my connecting flight out of Chicago, I sat next to a middle-aged man. I smiled and peppered him with questions, curious to hear his perspective and learn more about his family, his work, and what he was reading. My excitement overrode my ability to sense his growing annoyance. After a few moments, he gently but firmly interrupted me. "Wow, you sure love to ask questions of strangers. Are you a reporter?" I shook my head, saying I was just curious. "I'd like to get back to reading my book, if I may," he said with a half smile. When I realized my unmatched eagerness and finally read the situation accurately, I apologized. I had the right idea and the right motive, but it was the wrong time and with the wrong person.

Sometimes answers are needed. Other times, neither questions nor answers are warranted, just silence. Which is why, once again, wisdom is so important to the process. It's not just knowing what to ask and who to ask and why to ask. We also need to discern when to ask—or even whether to ask anything at all.

LIVING A QUESTION-ORIENTED LIFE

How do we ask questions and live into them?

The marvelous thing about a good question is that
it shapes our identity as much by the asking as
it does by the answering.

DAVID WHYTE

Who questions much, shall learn much, and retain much.

FRANCIS BACON

ON A WARM SUMMER FRIDAY NIGHT, friends gathered on the back patio of a Capitol Hill home in Washington, DC, for a night of steaks, jumbo shrimp, and good wine. A hooded intruder slid through an open gate, approached a fourteen-year-old girl, and put a gun to her head. "Give me your money or I'll start shooting." The five other guests, including the girl's parents, froze.

Amid the terror, Cristina Rowan blurted out the first thing that came to her mind: "We were just finishing dinner. Why don't you have a glass of wine with us?"

The intruder pulled the gun off the girl's head and slowly took a sip of their Château Malescot Saint-Exupéry.

"Damn, that's good wine."

The girl's father encouraged the intruder to take the whole glass, then offered him the bottle. He pulled his hood down and took another sip as well as a bite of the gourmet cheese on the table.

Tucking his handgun into the pocket of his sweatpants and looking around the patio, he said, "I think I may have come to the wrong house. I'm sorry. Can I get a hug?"

Rowan stood up and wrapped her arms around him. One by one, the four other guests stood up and embraced him.

"That's really good wine," the man said again, taking another sip. He had one final request: "Can we have a group hug?" The five adults surrounded and embraced him.

Then the man walked out with the crystal wineglass in hand, filled with more wine. No one was hurt; nothing was stolen. In the alley behind the home, investigators later found the intruder's empty crystal wineglass on the ground, unbroken.

The power of an unexpected question.

CHANGING THE QUESTION

If you change your questions, you change your life—and the lives of those around you. It would be great if we could toss any old question out into a conversation and experience a sense of kinship, but it rarely ever works that way. Growing in our ability and capacity to ask better questions, even questions we might blurt out in a harrowing situation during a dinner party, isn't merely about increasing the *quantity* of our questions. What we're after is improving their *quality*.

Enad is a medical student who grew up in the United Arab Emirates and attends our church. After the service ended on a cold January morning, a few of us were standing around talking when he mentioned he'd been excited over the past few days, as it was the first time in his life he had ever seen snow. We learned Enad had never thrown a snowball.

With snow still blanketing the ground, our group of five or six adults put our things down. "Come with us," we said.

We marched outside and participated in a friendly snowball fight. Enad smiled from ear to ear while he made his snowballs, giggling and shrieking when he got nailed and when he blasted others. He made a small snowman and learned how to make a snow angel. We all laughed until our stomachs hurt. It only lasted a few brief minutes, but it was a beautiful, soul-filling experience of joy.

Later I reflected on the experience. How did we learn that Enad had never thrown a snowball? I realized that instead of asking "How are you doing?" I had asked a more focused question: "What was your highlight of the past week?" In stretching myself to ask a better question, I had learned something about Enad. How many rich and joyful experiences have we missed because we asked bland and generic questions? How many more memories could we make and meaningful interactions could we have if we learned to ask better questions?

One simple way to improve the quality of our questions is to recognize the important difference between closed-ended and open-ended questions. Closed-ended questions seek a single answer, where the primary purpose is content. They often begin with *when, where, who, is, can*, and *do*. What time does your game start on Saturday? Where did you attend college? Do you like Brussels sprouts? It's like a zoom lens, focusing in on something with a small and concentrated perspective.

Open-ended questions hold the possibility of multiple answers, where the purpose is context. It's a wide-angle lens, capturing the full range of options and possibilities. These often begin with *why, what,* and *how.* How are you feeling about the big event you've been planning the past several months? What are you looking forward to the most this upcoming school year? What factors led your family to decide to go to Maine for vacation? The conversation could travel in a wide variety of directions. There certainly are advantages to both types of questions, but the quality of our questions often increases significantly when we ask more open-ended questions than closed-ended ones.

THE FOUR LEVELS OF GOOD QUESTIONS

There are direct and indirect questions. Open and closed questions. Generic and specific. Narrowing and expanding. Informative and emotive. Hypothetical and concrete. Rhetorical and reflective. Sarcastic and strategic. Stupid and naive. Affirming and scolding. Clarifying questions or ones used to intentionally confuse others. Loaded. Either-or. One-word questions—even silent questions. There are many types of questions, but not all are created equal.

I've developed a framework to help us think more carefully about questions. Good questions fall into four distinct levels, each level building upon the previous one. Once you understand the level of your questions, you can be more aware and thus more strategic in what you ask. The higher the level we climb, the higher the risk—and the higher the possibility for meaningful interaction. Additionally, the higher the level, the fewer people we can naturally ask those types of questions to.

But not all questions are good questions. Some are wounding, divisive, and narcissistic. *What's wrong with you? How could they be so stupid? How could anyone possibly vote for that person?* My father calls these Level Zero questions. They could also be described as Basement Questions, or maybe even Gutter Questions. These are not the kinds of questions I'm referring to. The four levels of questions imply ones that are intended for good and seek to be helpful.

Level One: Questions for information (simple facts). These questions are for the purpose of gaining more knowledge. They engage with simple facts in a transactional manner. These are the simplest, most natural, most straightforward questions that usually contain a clear answer. In most situations, though not all, you could approach a stranger and ask a Level One question without feeling any awkwardness in the interaction. It is entirely information transfer. They are almost always introductory, where almost all healthy relationships begin, and where both the questions and the answers are low risk.

- *What is your name?*
- *What time is it?*
- *What do you do for a living?*
- *Do you know what time the show begins?*
- *In what aisle would I find salad dressing?*

Level Two: Questions for interaction (thoughts and emotions). The intent of these questions is to get to know others relationally or to know the purpose behind something. They engage with thoughts and emotions. Level Two questions require at least some initial relational context and a bit of trust. This is where we seek to create empathy and express to others that we value what they think and feel. They are a bit deeper than Level One questions.

- *How are you doing lately?*
- *When did you first become interested in kayaking?*
- *How are you feeling going into today's meeting with your boss?*
- *What is the most rewarding and most difficult element of raising teenagers?*
- *On a scale of one to ten, how excited are you about launching that new project next month?*

Level One and Two questions are oftentimes where we engage in small talk. I don't want to bemoan small talk; it plays a unique role in our everyday interactions with others and can carry a cumulative effect. But if our conversations only remain at these levels, we won't be able to truly know and be known by others. We must look for the appropriate times to move past small talk to more substantive conversation.

Level Three: Questions for understanding (feelings and desires). The intent of these questions is to get to know others with a deeper level of engagement, which requires vulnerability. People often ask these questions where solid mutual trust is already established. Level Three questions engage with desires and passions. They invite people to open

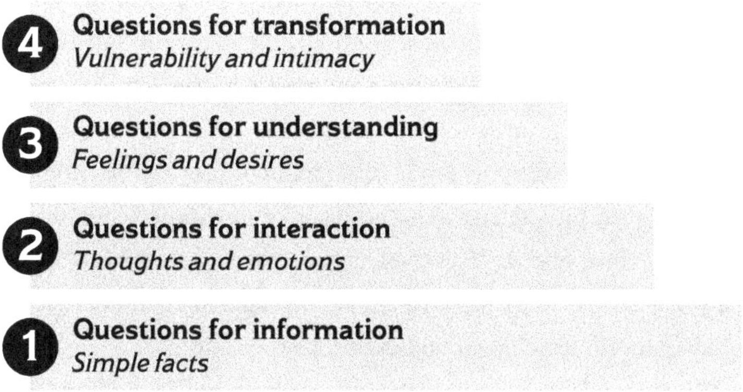

4 **Questions for transformation**
Vulnerability and intimacy

3 **Questions for understanding**
Feelings and desires

2 **Questions for interaction**
Thoughts and emotions

1 **Questions for information**
Simple facts

Figure 3.1. The four levels of good questions

up about their hopes, their dreams, and even their disappointments. This is the heart of where meaningful and healthy relationships reside. Whoever your close friends are, my guess is that you've forged those relationships the most at this level. It's where you've talked about the issues that matter most: a cancer diagnosis, a divorce, your promotion at work, the concern you hold for your child who's made destructive decisions. It's where others get to know the real you.

- *What do you want—really want—in your life?*
- *What breaks your heart?*
- *What are the fears that ultimately hold you back?*
- *What are you passionate about?*
- *What would you do if you weren't afraid of failing?*

When people engage effectively with Level Three questions, it creates a cycle that builds momentum. Asking questions about feelings, values, beliefs, and experiences nurtures healthy vulnerability. This then triggers emotional contagion, where others feel comfortable reciprocating appropriate vulnerability. This helps to cultivate a meaningful bond. Thus, emotional connection happens best at Level Three when people ask questions and reciprocate vulnerability.

Level Four: Questions for transformation (vulnerability and intimacy). These are questions that plumb the depths of our lives. It's where we open up our metaphorical underwear drawer and, as one of my friends from Texas says, where we get *soul-neked.* Because this level engages with the deepest point of human connection, peering deep into the most private and guarded parts of our souls, it requires immense amounts of trust. This level requires courageous vulnerability to truly be ourselves with others. It risks being hurt, but without it, it risks missing out on attachment and even transformation.

When we ask Level Four questions, we must be wise and tread carefully. We usually only have a small ring of people we engage with at this level. These may include a therapist, a spouse, a pastor or spiritual director, an accountability partner, and a few close lifelong friends. It's only when we are vulnerable that we grow—and Level Four questions are the most courageous, intimate, and vulnerable questions we can imagine asking and being asked.

- *When do you feel most fully seen? When do you feel most invisible?*
- *Can you identify your heart's cry right now, especially when there are tears present?*
- *What is it like on your darkest days, and how can I best love and support you in them?*
- *What would you want people to know right now that you might not have ever shared with others?*
- *What are you afraid to tell me (or others) in this moment?*

Another way to think about the four levels of questions is to compare it to how you enter the ocean. A Level One question is where you experience the ocean at an ankle-deep level. You are touched by the water, but you aren't immersed in it. A Level Two question puts you a bit farther out in thigh-deep water. A Level Three question is chest-deep; you're immersed in the water and feel the pull of the waves, yet your feet are still firmly touching the bottom. And a Level Four question is where you are swimming, fully immersed, no longer able to touch the bottom.

As we think about the framework, it's crucial to keep several things in mind.

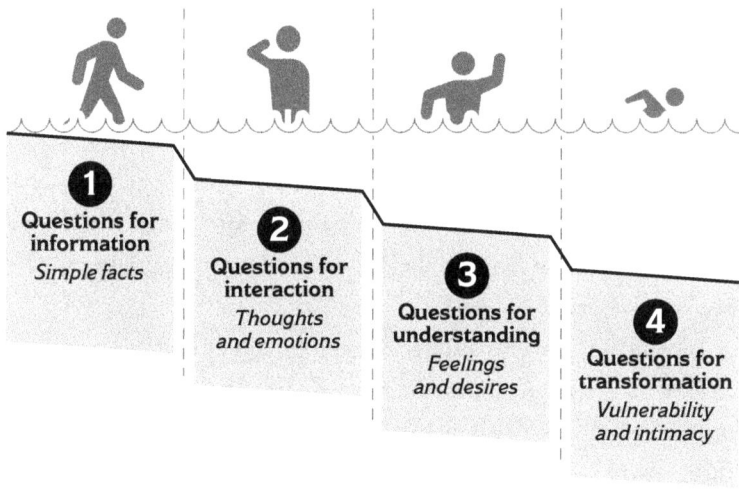

Figure 3.2. The four levels of good questions

First, we need wisdom to discern which question level is most appropriate in each interaction we have. If we think about our strongest relationships, they started out at Level One and progressed from there, but it didn't happen immediately. In fact, it happens over a period of time in almost every situation. If trust is developed at Level One, then people feel comfortable to move to Level Two and beyond. But we must be mindful to move at the speed of trust. Our deepest relationships—those where we feel most comfortable engaging in Level Four questions—most likely took several years, if not decades, to develop. But it's also in those relationships where we feel fully known and can most fully be ourselves.

Have you ever been in a situation where you were asked a question that felt awkward, embarrassing, or even a bit invasive? Your guard may have gone up and you felt a bit disoriented. Most likely it was a question asked at the wrong level of your current relationship. I can think of numerous examples when my eagerness and impatience to connect with someone overrode my wisdom in that moment, creating a cringeworthy situation.

If you sense that trust has *not* been clearly developed at your current level, it is wise to not move to the next level, at least not yet. Moving too quickly to the next level, or asking questions at a level that is out of order, can make the relational dynamic awkward. It risks an erosion of trust and an increase in suspicion. For example, approaching a stranger and asking, "So, when do you feel most fully loved?" isn't socially acceptable and would put that person immediately on edge. People only feel comfortable to move to the next level when appropriate trust has been established.

Second, we must also discern the appropriate cultural and contextual level of questions. At times, there are generational, geographical, and cultural forces at play that make asking questions less socially acceptable. Those who have a few more tree rings than others are generally more guarded about personal details of their lives than younger generations.

I grew up in the South and attended college in the Midwest, where I learned the unwritten yet clearly understood rule in both regions of the country: don't ask direct or personal questions, which is often perceived as intrusive, nosy, or rude. While these factors exist, I'm not suggesting that we should always acquiesce to the accepted and expected cultural norms of question levels. Instead, I'm suggesting that we possess equal measures of cultural sensitivity, wisdom, and courage to discern when and where we might appropriately lean in and look for ways to move conversations to another level.

Third, it's vitally important to understand that it's not the goal of every relationship to move to Level Four. It is appropriate—healthy even—for us to have relationships on all four levels. But are there people you've known for several years you don't know much about? You spend time together and end up talking about movies and sports and work trips and how you remodeled your downstairs bathroom, but beyond that, there's not much substance. It's because you've been hanging out almost entirely at Level One or Level Two for most of your relationship. There isn't much risk or vulnerability required to stay at those levels. If you long for deeper closeness with others, you'll need to draw on your courage and lean in to ask a next-level question.

Fourth, while it's important to be intentional and mindful of these levels in our relationships, we need to ensure we don't take a formulaic approach either. In doing so, we run the risk of squeezing the joy out of our interactions. Life-giving and meaningful relationships are to be enjoyed, not dissected. People can detect contrived and overstructured conversations quickly, which leads them to become suspicious and shut down. We don't want to force the petals of the rose buds open; instead, we want to cultivate healthy conditions by watering the rosebush and maintaining healthy pH levels in the soil so that the flowers bloom whenever they're ready.

Finally, now that we're cognizant of these levels, it's important to understand we don't have to ask questions every opportunity we can. Just because I love questions and am paid to ask them doesn't mean that I always ask people who sit next to me on flights or while standing in line at the coffee shop. There are times I don't ask because I sense they don't want to engage. And there are times when I just don't feel like it because I'm tired, or I'm not in the right head space or heart space. We need to be situationally aware.

Now, take a moment and consider the four levels of questions:

Can you think of a time from the past week or two when you asked a Level One question, like, "What time is the game on Saturday?"

When did you ask a Level Two question, such as, "What specific elements stuck out to you most from yesterday's presentation?"

On what kind of occasion did you ask a Level Three question, similar to, "What are your biggest fears as you think about making this important decision?"

When did you ask—or when did someone ask you—a rare but significant Level Four question, like, "What are you not confessing to me?"

ASKING IN AN AGE OF LONELINESS

In 1938, Harvard Medical School began a study attempting to find an answer to this question: What is the single most contributing factor to a happy life? This Harvard Grant Study, also known as the Study of Adult Development, is the longest research study ever conducted. It started more than eighty-five years ago and continues to this day. The report revealed that the single most important element to a good life is warm, intimate relationships. But there's a major problem: even with more access to information now than at any other time in history, we see more evidence of loneliness in the world than ever before.

Loneliness is an issue of ever-increasing concern today. Mother Teresa described it as the leprosy of the West. In 2018, UK prime minister Theresa May appointed Tracey Crouch as the first ever minister of loneliness to address the growing health issues created by social isolation. In efforts to curb the growing rise of suicide, Japan named their own minister in 2021. In 2017 it was also reported in Japan that an estimated four thousand people died alone without anyone's knowledge *each week*. Maybe that's why it's commonplace to rent pretend companions by the hour; the rent-a-friend business is booming. In his book *Together,* which ironically released the same month the world shut down from the global pandemic, US surgeon general Vivek Murthy called loneliness a public health crisis and declared it an epidemic in our country.

Before we're tempted to think that's a bit too extreme, consider this: loneliness is the single greatest risk factor for clinical depression. Members of Gen Z are posting friendship applications online. Many male students (and adults) are not only playing video games alone in their rooms, but they're also spending an exorbitant amount of time watching *strangers* play video games online. We are talking about loneliness honestly and openly, much more than we did a decade ago. While some may see it as a triumph of mental health awareness, it may be best understood as a public collective cry for help. Isolation and loneliness have contributed to an alarmingly high and ever-increasing rate of what are called deaths of despair.

I'm convinced: there has never been a time in modern history when genuine, thoughtful, caring questions are needed more. In a world saturated not only by ever-increasing loneliness but also by division, polarization, and fragmentation, genuine question-asking can provide healing and connection like almost nothing else.

THE IMPORTANT CONNECTION BETWEEN LISTENING AND QUESTIONS

Listening and question-asking are fraternal twins that share many features while still retaining their own distinct identities. The word *listen* is derived from two Anglo-Saxon words: *hlystan* ("hearing") and *hlosian* ("to wait in suspense"). This combination of words suggests we are not simply listening to what is being said; rather, we wait to absorb what is being said with thought, patience, and respect.

Many of us are fortunate enough to know that wonderful sense of truly being heard and known through a question asked, which is sustained by eye contact, an attentive posture, and follow-up questions. Listening remains the cornerstone of every relationship. Yet it's often misunderstood as simply doing nothing. Listening not only respects and values others, but it also enhances learning, reflects to others how they are thinking and feeling, demonstrates empathy, allows space for self-awareness, and creates ownership and responsibility. I love that the Chinese symbol for listening incorporates the symbols for the ear, the eyes, and the heart, a beautiful and clear reminder that the act requires whole-bodied engagement.

David Augsburger wrote that being heard is so close to being loved that, for the average person, they are almost indistinguishable. No wonder James, the half brother of Jesus, wrote that we "should be quick to listen, slow to speak, and slow to become angry" (Jas 1:19). We know it's important, yet many of us don't know how to do it. Imagine the implications if every high school and college required students to complete a course titled "How to Listen Well."

American socialite Jennie Jerome, also known as Lady Randolph Churchill (Winston Churchill's mother), recounted the time she dined with British politician Benjamin Disraeli and then, on a separate occasion, with his political rival William Gladstone. She wrote, "When I left the dining room after sitting next to Gladstone, I thought he was the cleverest man in England. But when I sat next to Disraeli, I left feeling that I was the cleverest woman." Of course, she preferred to spend time with Disraeli. Who wouldn't? While the two-time prime minister was a master orator, Disraeli was also an attentive listener who steered conversation away from himself and toward whoever he was with. As the adage goes, people don't care how much you know until they know how much you care. In a world filled with Gladstones, it's better to be a Disraeli.

Charles Derber, the Boston College sociologist mentioned earlier, has been studying the reasons and the effects of how our world longs for attention since the 1970s. He and his team launched the Attention-Interaction Project, where they recorded interactions and conversations with more than three hundred volunteers from various backgrounds. In the research, the team identified two kinds of responses: support-responses and shift-responses.

A shift-response shifts attention away from the speaker and toward the other person (Gladstone's approach). This is common among conversational narcissists, who squelch any further opportunity for mutual connection by diverting attention away from others and shining the spotlight onto themselves. It's like stealing the ball from someone else while they're dribbling. The approach stunts any opportunity for deeper understanding and intimacy; it's a *competitive interaction*.

Oftentimes, those who engage in shift-responses are what David Brooks dubs conversation toppers—those who are always trying to top the stories that others just shared. Few things kill the flow of conversation more than topping.

But a support-response keeps the attention focused on the speaker and what they are saying (Disraeli's approach). They encourage the speaker to elaborate further. The goal is to understand the speaker's point of view, not to sway it. Instead of walking into a room as if to announce, "Here I am," support-response people excitedly look at others as if to say, "There you are." These are *cooperative interactions*. It is an attention-giving posture that attempts to keep the conversation focused on the person who has just spoken.

Notice the different responses:

John: "My dog got out last week, and it took three days to find him."

Mary: "Our dog is always digging under the fence, so we can't let him out unless he's on a leash." (*shift-response*)

As opposed to: "Oh no, where did you finally find him?" (*support-response*)

or

Sue: "I watched this really good documentary about turtles last night."

Bob: "I'm not big on documentaries. I'm more of an action-film kind of guy." (*shift-response*)

As opposed to: "Turtles? How did you happen to see that? Are you into turtles?" (*support-response*)

A shift-response says, "Listen to me because I think I'm interesting," whereas a support-response says, "I'm listening to you because I'm interested." Shift-response people are Diminishers, while support-response people are Illuminators. In one of the bestselling books ever published, *How to Win Friends and Influence People,* Dale Carnegie wrote, "You can make more friends in two months by becoming interested in other people than you can in two years by trying to get other people interested in you." I've never heard a woman describe a first date saying, "The guy was such a turnoff. All he did was ask me thoughtful questions and genuinely listen to what I said." Have you? French social activist Simone Weil wrote, "Attention is the rarest and purest form of generosity." The word *attention* is a combination of two Latin words: *ad* ("to" or "toward") and *tendere* ("to stretch out or extend"). To pay attention to others is to have a posture of extending or stretching out toward them. As we show attention to others, we bless them in our extending—and we, too, are often blessed in the process.

The point is this: asking inviting, others-focused questions is the best, most practical way to remain in support-response mode. Therapy is an incredibly valuable tool that helps countless people process healthily and heal from difficult situations. But I wonder: *Would the world need as many therapists if we strove to be attentive and attuned support-response listeners?*

True, we need not always be in a support-response mode. Healthy relationships involve back-and-forth communication. We shouldn't just fire questions in someone's direction and refrain from sharing important elements of our own lives. That leaves the relationship one-sided. Conversely, if our neighbor shares with us that she's just gotten results back from the doctor indicating a cancer diagnosis, it would be perceived as unwise and uncaring to share about the pain in our lower back. That's a shift-response. However, when it is nuanced, we can learn to share our own vulnerability at appropriate times as a way of making an empathetic touchpoint, all the while keeping the focus on the other person and what they need in that moment.

Once you know about the shift-response/support-response dynamic, it's like the FedEx arrow: you can't unsee it. Or in this case, you *can't unhear it.* Listen to the conversations around you and you'll notice that the interactions are overwhelmingly shift-responses.

LISTENING AND QUESTIONS

It's possible to be good at listening but bad at asking questions. And I know people who ask good questions but are terrible listeners, interrupting and then quickly jumping into shift-response. We need both keen question-asking *and* active listening to care well for others. The interplay between listening and asking questions can be seen in figure 3.3.

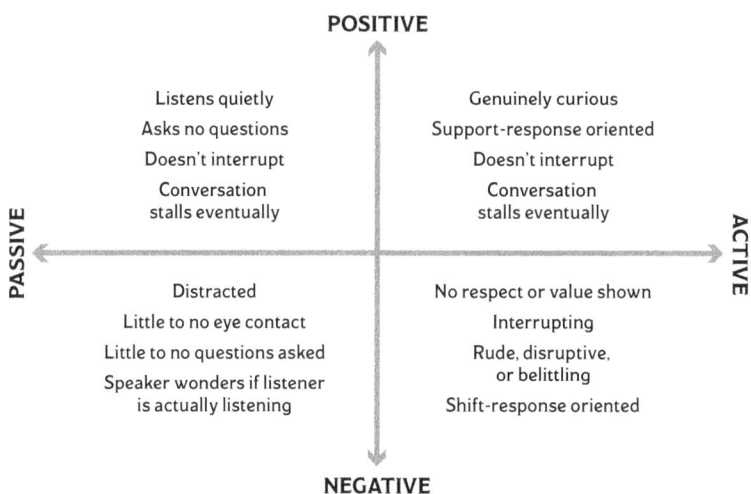

POSITIVE

Listens quietly	Genuinely curious
Asks no questions	Support-response oriented
Doesn't interrupt	Doesn't interrupt
Conversation stalls eventually	Conversation stalls eventually

PASSIVE ← → **ACTIVE**

Distracted	No respect or value shown
Little to no eye contact	Interrupting
Little to no questions asked	Rude, disruptive, or belittling
Speaker wonders if listener is actually listening	Shift-response oriented

NEGATIVE

Figure 3.3. The relationship between asking questions and listening

Listening and asking questions offer some benefit, but without any response, they encourage only one-way conversation. Asking questions and giving answers are at times beneficial, but without listening, they can easily usher in nothing more than mere information transference. Listening and responding provide some benefit, but without asking questions, they lead to the perception of an unequal dynamic. All three elements are required to maintain healthy and trustworthy relationships.

Questions are an important form of compassionate and generous hospitality. We often think of hospitality as taking a meal to a friend who was recently released from the hospital, hosting a barbecue, or inviting people over for dinner or drinks. All these are wonderful expressions, but they're not complete.

I've heard hospitality described as making people feel comfortable in a new environment. My friend Tim describes it as giving the privileges of insiders to outsiders, which means that asking questions may be one of the best ways to offer hospitality to others. Asking requires an appropriate release of control. It invites and encourages vulnerability, assuming an others-centered posture. By asking questions, we are tangibly embodying patience, kindness, and gentleness—a few generative elements of what Christians call the fruit of the Spirit.

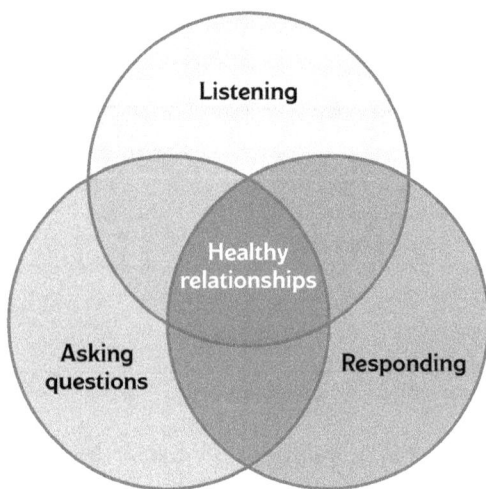

Figure 3.4. Diagram of elements that make up healthy relationships

There's a group of retired men in the YMCA locker room who catch up with each other as I'm getting dressed after a morning swim. They cover a wide variety of topics, but they aren't connecting; they're just waiting until someone else stops talking. They're impatiently waiting for their turn to share what they have planned for the day, how big the fish was they caught last week, or the golf outing they have planned later this month.

But there's one guy named Brendan. He's always asking thoughtful questions birthed out of genuine interest. He listens intently. He asks follow-up questions: "Do you guys have anything coming up on your schedules in the next few weeks you're looking forward to?" "You're heading up to Canada next week—what part?" "You caught a fish that large. Wow, what kind was it and where did you catch it?" He's a skilled Illuminator. Real John Stockton material, always looking to make the extra pass.

Want to be countercultural? Want to cultivate meaningful relationships with others? Be like Brendan. Excel in support-response in your interactions.

PART 2

EXPLORING QUESTIONS IN OUR SEARCH FOR FAITH

THE QUESTIONS WE ASK

What are the questions we ask—and why those?

Without questions, there is no learning.

W. EDWARDS DEMING

*It is not enough for me to ask the question; I want to
know how to answer the one question that seems to
encompass everything I face: What am I here for?*

RABBI ABRAHAM JOSHUA HESCHEL

AIRPORTS ARE FILLED WITH INVISIBLES—the hardworking and often unseen men and women who show up each
day for years on end to clean restrooms, push wheelchairs, and run cash
registers. Each one possesses a fascinating story, yet they remain vir-
tually invisible to travelers who scurry off to find their gate and then sit
and scroll on their phones until boarding begins. When I travel, I make
it a practice to acknowledge and interact with these often unseen yet
significant people. I learn something new from them, and they often
inspire me.

A few months ago on my way to catch a flight to Dallas, I was sitting
next to Tareq, the friendly shuttle driver for the offsite parking company
where I'd just left my car. I do this frequently enough at the Philadelphia

airport that I know it's about eight minutes from pickup at my car to drop-off at the terminal. After placing my rollaboard on the luggage rack and taking my seat, I asked Tareq if he was just starting his shift or about to be done for the day.

"Just started," he said with a thick Middle Eastern accent.

"Where are you from?" I asked.

"Iraq."

I asked him about his family, and he proudly told me that he had worked six days a week since 2009 driving this shuttle to save up enough money to pay for his two sons to go to college.

In slightly broken English, he said slowly, "Both of them graduate from Temple University few years ago."

"Congratulations," I told him. "You must be so proud."

He smiled again, but this time with tears in his eyes. "It's proudest things I done in my lifetime."

Now there were tears in mine.

When we arrived at the terminal, I grabbed my bag, handed him a tip, thanked him, and departed. A meaningful moment for both of us. *Eight minutes.*

Questions hold the immense power to humanize in the cracks and crevices of our days. How would we be able to share that moment together without them?

THE QUESTIONS WE ASK OURSELVES

There's an ancient story of a rabbi returning from a long day of studying Torah. It was later than usual, and the sun had almost set. Lost in prayerful thought, he arrived at a fork in the road, turning to travel left instead of his normal route home to the right. Coming to his senses, he realized he had not arrived home but was instead standing in front of a Roman outpost. A loud voice called out into the darkness, "Stop right there!" A Roman centurion stepped into view.

"Who are you and what are you doing here?" he barked.

The rabbi thought for a moment and replied, "How much are you paid to stand here each day?"

"Three drachma," said the soldier, slightly puzzled.

"I'll pay you twice as much if you stand at my front door and ask me those two questions every morning."

We need not hire a soldier to stand outside our house every day. But just imagine if we made it a regular practice to ask ourselves those questions of identity and purpose.

The quality of our lives is determined by the quality of the questions we ask God, ourselves, and others. And the questions we ask ourselves most often spill over into the types of questions we ask other people— our boss, our neighbors, our friends, our family members, strangers while standing in line at the post office, even Google.

Without even realizing it, we often ask ourselves three primary questions. They are the same three questions asked by humans for millennia: *Who is God? (Or the gods? Or is there a God or gods?) Who are we?* and *How do we live?* Put another way: *What is the meaning of life? What does it mean to be human?* and *What is the good life?* The Big Three are the driving force behind all religion, philosophy, education, art, and literature.

There's no escaping the big questions of life. In fact, we ask ourselves significant questions even before we know we are doing it. From birth, children are looking for answers to key questions of life: *Am I safe? How does love work? Am I worthy? Will I be cared for?* When we are babies, our minds and bodies internalize answers to those questions based on what we see around us and how we are treated by others. What is most fascinating is that all of this happens *even though later, as adults, we have no conscious memory of this period.* The desire to ask questions is hardwired into our DNA, especially as children. We can't help but ask ourselves questions.

The late Rabbi Jonathan Sacks wrote:

> One reason religion has survived in the modern world despite four centuries of secularization is that it answers the three

questions every reflective human being will ask at some time in his or her life: Who am I? Why am I here? How then shall I live? These cannot be answered by the four great institutions of the modern West: science, technology, the market economy, and the liberal democratic state. Science tells us how but not why. Technology gives us power but cannot tell us how to use that power. The market gives us choices but does not tell us which choices to make. The liberal democratic state as a matter of principle holds back from endorsing any particular way of life. The result is that contemporary culture sets before us an almost infinite range of possibilities, but does not tell us who we are, why we are here, and how we should live.

Who am I? Why am I here? How then shall I live? They sound like variations of the Big Three, don't they? They drive many—if not most—of our motivations, our hopes, our fears, our understanding of our identity, our desires, and our deepest longings. These are the questions that help shape who we are.

Part of what makes us human is our capacity to ask ourselves questions. No animal or species on earth has this capacity. Lutheran pastor and anti-Nazi dissident Dietrich Bonhoeffer reflected on his life's purpose from his prison cell in Tegel in the summer of 1944, several months before he died. He wrote a poem titled "Who Am I?" in which he wrestled with his identity. Was his identity based on what he experienced, what others said of him, or what God thought about him? Even Nietzsche's famous quote—"He who has a why to live can bear almost any how"—is based on the questions we ask. Could this be what the author of Ecclesiastes meant when he said that God has placed eternity in the hearts of people (Eccles 3:11)?

Questions are so deeply ingrained in the human experience that even the *absence* of questions—or answers to those questions—can tell us something significant about the state of our minds and souls. One diagnostic tool utilized by mental health professionals to help identify depression in patients is to ask, "What is one thing you desire to be doing in ten years?" If patients are unable to answer, this can often be a sign that depression has taken up residence in their life.

THE QUESTIONS OF OUR INNER VOICE

As we grow older, many of us, though not all, become more aware of an inner voice that talks to us, encouraging, scolding, and reminding us of what is true (and, at times, trying to convince us of things that are also untrue). We are constantly talking to ourselves. It can be helpful, and it can drive us crazy. It's like an incessant life coach who follows us around, whispering things at all hours of the day. Our verbal stream of thought is so constant and prolific that, according to one study, we internally talk to ourselves at a rate equivalent to *speaking four thousand words per minute out loud*. To put this in perspective, that is about 320 State of the Union addresses every single day. We can't fire or evict that inner voice in our heads, no matter how hard we may try. Instead, we must learn to have a right relationship with it. It's not only important; it's necessary.

THE SEVEN PRIMAL QUESTIONS (BY MIKE FOSTER)

We all have a driving question behind who we are and why we do what we do. Our primal question reveals our apex emotional need. When it's not met, we aren't the best versions of ourselves. We've been stamped with a primal question since our childhood—and as adults, we subconsciously and repeatedly ask it. Whatever your question is, it's so normal to you that you assume everyone is as preoccupied with the question as you are.

When the answer to our question is yes, we feel safe and positive, but when the answer is no or maybe, we enter what Foster calls "the scramble," like someone has just shaken up our emotional snow globe.

The Seven Primal Questions:

1. *Am I safe?* The need: physical and emotional safety.
2. *Am I secure?* The need: financial and relational security.
3. *Am I loved?* The need: to be known, seen, and emotionally attached with others.

4. *Am I wanted?* The need: to feel accepted, to belong, to be pursued.
5. *Am I successful?* The need: to succeed.
6. *Am I good enough?* The need: to be valued and affirmed for who we are.
7. *Do I have a purpose?* The need: significance and impact.

What questions does your inner voice ask frequently? Which questions are worth paying attention to, and which ones would be wise to ignore? The important challenge is to train ourselves to recognize the questions and then ask better questions—*the right kinds* of questions—of ourselves. There is a synergistic relationship between questions and reflection. Both are needed. Questions help us to reflect better, and reflection helps us to ask better questions of ourselves. Engaging with them well induces a flywheel effect.

Questions shape our posture and approach in our spirituality. What we ask and *when* we ask hold significant implications for our way of thinking and living. Longtime pastor and author Gordon MacDonald believes that we ask different questions as we grow older. In his book *A Resilient Life,* he writes:

> You won't be asking the same questions ten years from now that you are asking about your life today. . . . And as the questions change, so does the content of our spiritual interests. The questions often become our way of approach when we go to the Scriptures looking for spiritual sustenance. They become a guide when we buy books. The questions form our approach to spiritual life. So if the way one does spiritual life was formed around twenty-something questions, and one is now fifty, spiritual life will likely be obsolete and ineffective.

Over the years, few resources have been more helpful in my personal reflection and development than MacDonald's questions framework for each decade of life. It named what I had been feeling through each decade, helping me to feel far less alone and more understood. I share them with friends and leaders I serve who are attempting to navigate the choppy waters of growing older. I've included his list of questions in the back of the book in Resource 2.

OUR QUESTIONS AND OUR DECISIONS

The questions we ask ourselves drive not just our thoughts about faith and identity but also our decision-making. Before making a significant decision, many people frequently generate a traditional pros and cons list: *What is the best- and worst-case scenario here?* Former General Electric CEO Jack Welch developed a decision-making matrix that helps us to gain perspective by thinking in three different time frames: *How will I feel about this ten minutes from now? How will I feel about this ten months from now? How will I feel about this ten years from now?* It provides needed perspective. When the right questions are present, oftentimes the answer naturally appears.

Ultimately, when we train our minds to ask better, wiser, more focused questions, we begin to think more clearly and discerningly. The wisest people I know are constantly asking themselves questions related to their past, present, and future perspective, the risks involved, if it aligns with their values and principles, and what is of ultimate importance to them. When we ask ourselves the right questions at the right time for the right reason, and then act accordingly, we become wiser and more self-aware. We make better decisions.

MacDonald and his wife, Gail, compiled a list of hard-hitting reflection questions they ask themselves regularly:

- *Am I too defensive when asked questions about the use of my time and the consistency of my spiritual disciplines?*
- *Have I locked myself into a schedule that provides no rest or fun times with friends and family?*
- *What does my schedule say about time for study, general reading, and bodily exercise?*

- *What about the quality of my speech? Do I whine and complain? Am I frequently critical of people and institutions or of those who clearly do not like me?*

- *Am I drawn to entertainment that does not reflect my desired spiritual culture?*

- *Am I tempted to stretch the truth, enlarge numbers that are favorable to me, or tell stories that make me look good?*

- *Do I blame others for things that are my own fault or the result of my own choices?*

- *Is my spirit in a state of quiet so I can hear God speak?*

Interacting frequently with questions like these is how we cultivate a life of wisdom, where we understand our true identity and grow to make better decisions.

THE QUESTIONS WE ASK OTHERS

Asking good questions of others requires us to ask thoughtful questions of ourselves first. When he was twenty-five years old, Nick moved to Denver to pursue a master's degree and to be close to one of his mentors. Even though he was doing what he knew he was called to do and what he had long looked forward to doing, he realized after a few months that he wasn't enjoying himself and had become increasingly frustrated.

The previous year, he'd been forced to face several troubling parts of his life, which led to an identity crisis—all in a short amount of time. He was perpetually tired and found himself in constant physical pain, though he didn't have a good reason why. Everything was a slog. In one of the weekly meetings with his mentor, he asked Nick, "When was the last time you experienced joy?" and told Nick to take as long as he wanted to answer. Reflecting on the situation years later, Nick shared with me, "I felt relieved, because it was such a simple question. I'd been expecting a really difficult question. I tried to remember . . . but I just couldn't. It was the most agonizing three minutes of my life. I honestly didn't even know what joy was in my experience anymore."

His mentor let the silence remain long enough for Nick to tearfully admit he couldn't remember.

"I know," his mentor assured him. "Now it's time to get you some help." He helped Nick connect to a doctor, which led to a diagnosis of clinical depression. Nick spent the next three years digging his way out with the help of friends, family, and medication. "The question saved my life," he shared, "and gave me the diagnostic of joy that I've used ever since to ensure my wings are level and the nose is up."

Asking great questions of others holds immense possibility to nurture connection. Great questions open doors to beautiful and honest conversations about what truly matters. They can highlight important issues and create strong bonds of trust. And they can usher in awareness to save someone's life. But Nick's mentor first had to ask himself a set of thoughtful questions before he asked Nick—questions such as, *Nick does not seem himself. I wonder: When was the last time he experienced joy? What might Nick need to be healthy and joyful again?*

QUESTIONS FROM DAVID BROOKS (FROM *HOW TO KNOW A PERSON*)

What's your favorite unimportant thing about you?

What crossroads are you at?

If the next five years is a chapter in your life, what is the chapter about?

Can you be yourself where you are and still fit in?

What would you do if you weren't afraid?

If you died today, what would you regret not doing?

What have you said yes to that you no longer really believe in?

What is the no, or refusal, you keep postponing?

What is the gift you currently hold in exile? (In other words, what talent are you not using?)

Why you? (As in, why was it you who started that business? Why was it you who ran for school board?)

As we explored earlier, asking questions doesn't come naturally due to a myriad of cultural forces pushing against us. Sadly, self-centered thinking is the dominant position in our age and is often celebrated. David Brooks writes that our world excitedly encourages people to see themselves as the center of their universe. He estimates that about 30 to 40 percent of people are good question-askers. I think that number is much too high. (Try this experiment: next time you're at a social gathering, look around and ask yourself, *Who here is asking the most thoughtful, engaging, and meaningful questions?* It's harder than you might think.)

When a young student is upset, some teachers have learned to ask, "Do you want to be helped, hugged, or heard?" That's a fantastic question—and not just for students. Why? Because different needs and desires require different responses. Those three types require different kinds of engagement. If we can step back to ask ourselves, *What is this conversation really about?* and *What's really going on here?* then we can discern if others desire a practical problem-solving approach (to be helped), an empathetic response (to be hugged), or if they need someone to listen and validate their experience (to be heard). Knowing the difference makes all the difference. You show me a person of depth, warmth, and wisdom, and I'll show you someone who's learned to ask thoughtful and meaningful questions of themselves and others.

My wife and I were invited to a dinner party at the home of a devout Muslim couple. The spread of food was incredible and their hospitality warm and inviting. It was a fascinating arrangement of a few dozen folks from a wide variety of faiths—Christians, Muslims, Jews, Mormons, and atheists—for a wonderful Middle Eastern meal. As we all sat around our tables and asked questions, I noticed how the group focused less on religious differences and more on everyday elements of life. We asked each other questions about our dreams and shared our favorite cities in the world, where we'd like to travel to next, and what gives each of us meaning and fulfillment in our careers. It was one of those rare occasions where I could look around and see that almost everyone there was asking thoughtful questions with an evident posture of a support-response. It was such a rich night of interaction and conversation over amazing food. I remember sitting back and thinking, *This is what happens when people are genuinely curious and seek to lean in and ask meaningful questions.*

5

THE GOD WHO ASKS

If God knows everything, why does he ask questions?

Oh my soul . . . be prepared for him who knows how to ask questions.

T. S. ELIOT

My God . . . while I am asking questions which You do not answer, you ask me a question which is so simple that I cannot answer. I do not even understand the question.

THOMAS MERTON

WE'VE BEEN EXPLORING the work of questions in our lives and in our interactions with others. But now let's turn to the role of questions as we engage with God. How do our questions shape our faith—and how does our faith shape our questions?

Why would an all-knowing, all-capable God, who created every detail of the universe and holds every ounce of knowledge available in the world, ask questions at all? Why would he ask if he needs no answers? If you've ever wondered this, you're not alone. The Jewish philosopher Philo of Alexandria pondered this way back in the first century. The Christian faith affirms that God asks for much the same reason as we do: he desires a relationship with people. God's nature is fundamentally relational, and his questions invite people further into relationship and an ever-deepening intimacy with him.

Commands and demands are most often stated in the form of a monologue—and God most certainly communicates with his creation this way. But God's questions cultivate the conditions for conversation and relationship. God does not pose questions because he lacks knowledge but to show vulnerability to be in closer relationship with creation. Formation, not information.

Trevor Hudson writes that God knows questions create a deeper impact and transform us more than if he simply provides all the answers. He's the one who created questions in the first place. In immense humility, he asks so we can learn and discover ourselves. Questions are a tool God uses to drive us beyond the superficial and the comfortable. God wants all of creation to know he values what we think and feel.

When God asked Adam and Eve in the Garden, "Where are you?" (Gen 3:9), learning their exact physical location was not his intent. It is not a geographical and spatial question; it is a relational and theological question. He was seeking to draw them out of hiding. The question was not for the benefit of God, but for Adam and Eve. While God was asking Adam, it is also as if he's asking us as readers, "Where are we relationally? What is our status?" Pastor Gino Geraci offers an insightful perspective: the tone in which we hear God ask Adam, "Where are you?" says a great deal about how we view him.

This hit me several years ago while playing hide-and-seek with my two young sons. I could see their little fingers and toes sticking out from under a chair in the corner of our living room. I knew exactly where they were. Yet I still asked with a lilting tone of anticipation, drawing out the question for effect, "Where are you?" Each time, they could not contain their giggles. Why? Because there is joy in knowing someone who loves you is pursuing you. While I'm certain Adam felt quite differently at hearing God's question than my sons did when I asked mine, our intent was the same: to draw them out from their hiding in order to connect.

WHY QUESTION-ASKING REFLECTS THE HEART OF GOD

As I've studied the questions of Scripture extensively, people frequently ask me how many questions there are in the Bible. My answer often disappoints them because, well, it's hard to say exactly. Translating from the original languages to modern-day English is a complicated and nuanced endeavor. While we can't land on an exact number of questions God asked, we can arrive confidently at this: God cares about questions. He asks a lot of them. God's message and mission are participation oriented. God does not simply want to speak while people idly and passively listen. Participation equals value. God longs for participants in his story—and what better way to do that than to ask questions?

God loves asking rhetorical questions. Some of them are quite unsettling. After God asked Adam and Eve, he confronted everyone from patriarchs and prophets to judges and kings. Just as parents ask their kids rhetorical questions to force them to think and to take responsibility for their actions, God does this with his people. When God asks humans a rhetorical question, he expects a response. In fact, divine questions demand responses because an omniscient God has no need to ask them in the first place.

After Adam and Eve's fateful decision, God did not offer statements or commands at first. He could have asked what we might expect him to ask: "Why are you hiding?" But he didn't. It's possible Adam was expecting God to ask this question, because it's actually the question he answered. God continued to ask the couple, "Who told you that you were naked? Have you eaten from the tree that I commanded you not to eat from?" (Gen 3:11) and "What is this you have done?" (Gen 3:13). Later, God asked a pregnant, runaway Egyptian slave girl, "Hagar, slave of Sarai, where have you come from, and where are you going?" (Gen 16:8). God asked the depressed prophet, "What are you doing here, Elijah?" (1 Kings 19:9). These questions are not geographical in nature but relational and spiritual.

Or take the three visitors who arrived unexpectedly at the tent of Abraham and Sarah, who were well advanced in age. The visitors informed the couple that in one year's time they would have a son. Upon overhearing this, Sarah laughed to herself. The Lord asked, "Why did Sarah laugh and say, 'Will I really have a child, now that I am old?' Is anything too hard for the LORD?" (Gen 18:13-14). Is there another question he could have asked that would have gotten to the heart of faith as quickly and directly as that one? This calls us to pause and consider: *Is God willing and able to keep his promises, even in seemingly impossible situations?*

And what about his puzzling question to Jacob in Genesis 32? Jacob wrestled with a man of God through the night on the banks of the Jabbok River, having his hip wrenched from its socket in the process. Wrestling until daybreak would have left Jacob utterly exhausted, I would imagine. Jacob replied he would not let him go until the man blessed him. The man of God asked Jacob directly, "What is your name?" (Gen 32:27). After Jacob answered, the man told him his name would no longer be Jacob but Israel: "one who wrestles with God." Certainly, the man of God would have known his name, but he asked as a way to mark the moment indelibly for Jacob and for the nation of Israel. Conversely, Jacob requested God's name, to which God responded by asking another question—"Why do you ask my name?"—and then blessed Israel. Why so mysterious?

God appeared to Moses in the wilderness as a burning bush and informed him of his mission to lead God's people, the nation of Israel, out of Egypt and into the Promised Land. Riddled with self-doubt, Moses responded with deep insecurity. God asked, "What is that in your hand?" (Ex 4:2). Moses replied it was his staff. God told him to throw it down on the ground and turned it into a snake; then he told

Moses to pick the snake up by its tail. When Moses did, the snake returned to its original form: a staff. God intended for questions to set the stage for an experiential lesson, which marked Moses' leadership for the remainder of his life.

But this was not the end of Moses' doubting—nor was it the end of God's questions for him. In Numbers 11, the Israelites complain about their hardships in the wilderness, arousing God's anger. Despite God's daily and sufficient provision of manna in the wilderness, the people longed for meat. Moses complained to God, *asking six successive questions*, blaming God for the people's complaining (Num 11:11-14). Moses continued with more questions, to which God responded in a striking manner: "Is the LORD's arm too short? Now you will see whether or not what I say will come true for you" (Num 11:23). Delivering on this promise, a divine wind drove quail inland from the sea and scattered them all along the wilderness floor, providing meat for the Israelites and amply satisfying the wants of the people (Num 11:32-33). Amid my own doubt, I often ask myself that question to bolster my faith: *Is the Lord's arm too short?*

Or how about the hilariously bizarre and slightly unnerving story in Numbers 22 in which God caused a donkey to speak discernible words to get Balaam's attention? God asked, "Why have you beaten your donkey?" (Num 22:32). In the midst of miscommunication, hidden motivations, disobedience—and to top it all off, a talking animal—God's questions brought about another significant experiential lesson for Balaam. When questions start coming out of your ass, you know you're in trouble.

And what about Joshua? As faithful a leader as Joshua was, he was quick to blame God when the invasion of Ai failed. God asked him, "What are you doing down on your face?" (Josh 7:10). Joshua cried out, "Alas, Sovereign LORD, why did you ever bring this people across the Jordan to deliver us into the hands of the Amorites to destroy us?" (Josh 7:7). God's question not only invited dialogue and interaction, but it also called Joshua into action and participation in what God desired from him—and challenged him to deeper trust.

In Judges 6, through the presence of an angel, God spoke to Gideon: "The LORD is with you, mighty warrior" (Judg 6:12). Gideon, confused by this statement, asked, "Pardon me, my lord, but if the LORD is with us, why has all this happened to us?" (Judg 6:13). God responded with a command: "Go in the strength you have and save Israel out of Midian's hand. Am I not sending you?" (Judg 6:14). God's rhetorical question to Gideon was both a command and an invitation.

And what are we to make of Jonah's questions? The book of Jonah features two deeply compelling questions from God. If you grew up attending Sunday school or Vacation Bible School, you may have been led to believe that the book is about the prophet Jonah and the great big fish. But ultimately, the book is more concerned with a complaining prophet and a wildly compassionate God. The great irony of the book is that everyone and everything in the book of Jonah changes—the pagan sailors, the fish, the storm, the vine, the wind, the Ninevites, even the pagan king himself—except for Jonah. He became angry because God cared for the city of Nineveh when Jonah was convinced the city should be destroyed. God relented and showed mercy and compassion to the Ninevites. Jonah became unhinged.

In chapter 4, he was so angry he told God he wanted to die. God replied, "Is it right for you to be angry?" (Jon 4:4). Jonah gave no answer—at least not at first. Jonah sat down east of the city, and the Lord graciously provided a vine to grow and shield him from the heat. Then a worm chewed the vine, and it withered and died. Once again, Jonah became angry and expressed his desire to die, to which God asked a second time: "Is it right for you to be angry about the plant?" (Jon 4:9).

And Jonah had the audacity to reply emphatically that yes, it was. In fact, he was so angry he wanted to die.

The book concludes not with a statement but with a rhetorical question: "Should I not have concern for the great city of Nineveh, in which there are more than a hundred and twenty thousand people who cannot tell their right hand from their left—and also many animals?" (Jon 4:11). How did Jonah respond? We don't know. It's a cliffhanger. But the beauty and power of God's question is that it also forces us, the reader, to ponder our answer.

Then there's Job, of course. The book of Job contains the most questions of any book in the Bible—more than three hundred. Different characters ask questions in this book. Satan asks, "Does Job fear God for nothing?" (Job 1:9). In chapter 3, Job asks six different *why* questions, including, "Why did I not perish at birth, and die as I came from the womb?" (Job 3:11). The bulk of the book covers the responses of Job's friends, who essentially ask him, "God wouldn't let the righteous suffer like this, would he?"

The most arresting use of rhetorical questions in the Old Testament comes when God asks Job a whole laundry list of them. Despite being a righteous, faith-filled man, Job questions God in the midst of immense suffering. I'm certain we would as well if we were in his shoes. Job says earlier in the book, "Let the Almighty answer me" (Job 31:35). And oh, does God answer. He unleashes a slew of rhetorical questions in unrelenting succession.

In the climax of the book, he appears to Job out of the whirlwind and asks a brazen question, followed by a challenge: "Who is this that obscures my plans with words without knowledge? Brace yourself like a man; I will question you, and you shall answer me" (Job 38:2-3). Job experiences God's power and mystery in a series of rhetorical questions—*over sixty of them spanning five chapters* (Job 38–42). Some are brief: "Where were you when I laid the earth's foundation? Tell me, if you understand." (Job 38:4). Other questions are so blunt and forceful they span four verses (Job 38:8-11). God reminds Job in no uncertain terms that it is he who created all, rules all, and continues to be in control of all. God does as he pleases.

God made no attempt to answer Job's specific charges against him, nor did he provide satisfactory answers to Job. Rather, this situation confirmed Job's lack of knowledge about why he had suffered. God stressed the limitations of Job's wisdom by firing questions at him that were impossible to answer. It was forceful and clear that Job could do nothing else but plead ignorance. When God finished his whirlwind of questions, Job was overwhelmed by God's power and mystery. Humbled, there was only one thing left he could do: he repented.

And while it succeeded in restoring Job's trust in the wisdom, goodness, and power of God, *Job never received a direct answer to his questions.* Instead, God offered his presence and reminded Job of his mystery, vastness, and power. God chose to ask questions to connect with his creation and reveal the immensity of his power.

The good news is this: he still chooses to ask us questions, even today. I often hear from God in the form of questions. Sometimes they are comforting: *Do you know how much I love you?* Sometimes they are reminders: *Have you forgotten that my grace is sufficient for you and my mercies are new every morning? Have I ever been unfaithful to you or anyone else?* Sometimes they are challenges: *Will you trust me? Will you remember my goodness in the difficult, uncertain, and painful times?* And other times they are confronting and disturbing: *Do you know how much your stubbornness and disobedience hurt me? When will you go make things right with your wife and ask for her forgiveness?*

God sees questions as an opportunity for deeper relationship. It's no wonder he asks so many of them. He is the God who asks.

And that raises a whole new set of questions.

6

THE QUESTIONS JESUS ASKS

Why did the Way, the Truth,
and the Life ask questions?

What do you think?

Jesus (Mt 18:12)

Jesus answered them with a question.

Mark 10:3 NLT

HAVE YOU EVER NOTICED how often Jesus formed and transformed people by taking them on three kinds of field trips?

First, he took his listeners on *literal field trips.* I find it interesting how often Jesus' teachings occurred outside of a formal classroom setting and within the context of real life. As they walked on the way, he told his followers to look at the birds of the air and see the lilies of the field. He took them people-watching in the temple, where they observed a widow drop in two mites—and then he seized the teachable moment. Jesus knew that we learn when our bodies are fully engaged and out in the real world.

Jesus also took people on *emotional field trips.* He told stories. Even at the youngest age, we long for stories. The human brain processes forty thoughts per second when listening to a story. Reading stories essentially simulates reality in readers' brains, just as computer simulations run on computers. We sit in a dark theater watching a film that transports us to another world. At times we are overcome with immense fear or break out in uncontainable laughter. We may finish a novel and weep uncontrollably. Jesus knows how the human heart is wired for and moved by story. His parables engaged people's hearts and still engage today. He knew stories moved people in ways that facts, stats, and data simply could not do. Stories are so crucial to the human spirit that whoever tells the best stories wins the culture. Jesus' stories had a question baked into each of them: *What do you think?*

And Jesus took people on *mental field trips*, which occurred primarily through questions. His questions, like his stories, forced people to think on their own, take a stand, and decide. This particular field trip, of course, is the central focus of this book.

Jesus knew we learn and are formed best in experiences, stories, and questions. And yet, I frequently meet with and coach several pastors who lament that nobody in their church is changing or growing. I point out the irony that church structures often involve sitting people in a sanctuary, supplying abstract facts, and preaching by giving them answers rather than asking questions—the complete opposite approach to Jesus' three field trips. Might there be more opportunities for growth and transformation if we considered adapting our approach and engaging others the way Jesus did?

Some of my favorite conversations have been with rabbis. Quite predictably, within a moment or two of conversation, they either start to tell a story or ask a thoughtful question. It's a part of their rabbinic training. So it should come as no surprise that Jesus, a rabbi, did the same thing with his listeners. Several years ago, I was struck by a question that wouldn't leave me: *If Jesus asked so many great questions, why wouldn't I study the way he asked them—and then, in turn, learn to ask questions like he did?* The deeper I dug into these field trips, especially mental field trips, the more amazed I became. I couldn't ignore the frequency, primacy, and piercing force of his questions. They messed with me. They still do. They were often surprising, unpredictable, and enigmatic. Several times Jesus would ask questions that made people look at each other and scratch their heads, but they always made people think.

THE CENTRALITY OF QUESTIONS IN JESUS' LIFE

Let's take a deep dive into the questions of Rabbi Jesus. Over the past several years I've come to realize just how central questions were to Jesus' life and teachings. The first words of Jesus recorded in the Gospels are questions. In the Gospel of Luke, Mary and Joseph lost track of their twelve-year-old son on the way home from the temple. They returned to Jerusalem presumably on the verge of a panic attack and found him in the temple in discussion with the religious experts of the law. What was he doing when they found him? Sitting with the religious teachers listening to them and *asking questions*—and the teachers were amazed by him (Lk 2:46-47).

The first thing Mary did when she found Jesus, full of relief and indignation like any parent in that situation, was to ask him a question: "Son, why have you treated us like this?" (Lk 2:48). Jesus moved from asking questions of the religious teachers to asking his mother, not just one question but two: "Why were you searching for me? . . . Didn't you know I had to be in my Father's house?" (Lk 2:49). On the surface, Jesus' first question seems flippant. Every mother would be looking for her lost son, and she had been looking *for the past three days*. The second registers as a bit blunt: "Where'd you think you'd find me, Mom?" And yet, his two questions are theologically profound. Even Jesus' questions, as a middle schooler, speak of the vision of his earthly ministry.

In Jesus' teaching in the Sermon on the Mount, he asked seventeen questions—almost all of them rhetorical. During his ministry, Jesus poked at his listeners' most fundamental longings. When they properly recognized them, they grasped that these longings pointed to God. But most of his questions were conversational in nature.

The Gospel of John records over fifty questions of Jesus.

At the end of Jesus' life, some of his last words on the cross were a question: "My God, my God, why have you forsaken me?" (Mt 27:46; Mk 15:34).

Even after he was raised from the dead, he still asked questions: "Woman, why are you weeping? Who is it you are looking for?" (Jn 20:15).

He asked his disciples, "Friends, haven't you any fish?" (Jn 21:5).

On the road to Emmaus, he acted naive by asking, "What are you discussing together as you walk along?" (Lk 24:17).

He asked Peter three different times, "Do you love me?" (Jn 21:15-17).

THE SIX REASONS JESUS ASKED LOTS OF QUESTIONS

In the previous chapter we explored why the all-knowing God would ask questions. *But why did Jesus ask?* I can identify six different reasons.

1. Honor and dignity. In Mark 5, we read that Jesus and his disciples sailed from the western side of the Sea of Galilee across to the eastern side to find a dangerous and scary man possessed by a legion of demons who had terrorized local residents. Jesus saw the man and did something in that interaction that few of us would do. He asked the man a question: "What is your name?" (Mk 5:9). Like his Father, Jesus wasn't looking to gain more information; he desired to extend compassion along the lines of relationship. His questions often brought honor and restored people's dignity.

2. Redemption and compassion. A few verses later, Jesus walked through a crowded section of town. People pushed and jostled for the opportunity to get near him. Jesus suddenly stopped, turned around, and asked, "Who touched my clothes?" (Mk 5:30). I can imagine Peter turning to one of the disciples and saying under his breath, "Are you kidding me? What kind of question is that? *Everyone* is touching him!"

It was in that moment a trembling woman fell before Jesus' feet. According to Jewish custom, in her physical condition she shouldn't have even been in a crowded place near people, running the risk of accidentally brushing up next to someone and making them ceremonially unclean. But instead of scolding her for making him unclean by her touch, Jesus blessed her, healed her, and honored her desperate faith. Jesus, of course, knew who touched him. But had he not asked that question he would not have had the opportunity to honor the woman and create such a redemptive moment of grace.

3. Lessons and confrontations. On four different occasions Jesus asked his listeners, "What do you think?" (Mt 17:25; 18:12; 21:28; 22:42). In one situation, Jesus was among some self-satisfied religious experts who were confident they could trap Jesus with a crafty question: "Is it right to pay the imperial tax to Caesar or not? Should we pay or shouldn't we?" (Mk 12:14-15). Fittingly, Jesus responded to the question with a question: "Why are you trying to trap me?" (Mk 12:15). He requested a coin and then asked whose image and inscription were on it.

He wasn't asking for knowledge; every first-century Jew would have known the answer. He was asking for effect. The Jewish leaders forbade anyone from having a graven image of any person within the temple area. But there it was, right there in front of them: Caesar's image engraved on that coin. Jesus turned the tables, catching them in their hypocritical argument. His two questions—"Whose image is this? And whose inscription?" (Mt 22:19)—put the ball on the tee. "'Caesar's,' they replied." Then he crushed the ball right down the middle of the fairway: "Give back to Caesar what is Caesar's and to God what is God's" (Mk 12:17). It was a lesson those religious leaders most assuredly never forgot.

4. Reframing questions and challenging assumptions. When Jesus entered the temple courts, the religious leaders came to him, this time questioning his authority. "By what authority are you doing these things? And who gave you this authority?" (Mt 21:23). He challenged them. *Okay. Answer my question, I'll answer yours.* "John's baptism—where did it come from? Was it from heaven, or of human origin?" (Mt 21:25). They had tried to trap Jesus; now Jesus put them in a Gordian knot and trapped them back. All they could do to save face was to admit they didn't know (and oh, they knew all right). So Jesus replied, "Neither will I tell you by what authority I am doing these things" (Mt 21:27). He didn't say, "I don't know either." He simply acknowledged that if they couldn't name what everyone knew was the answer, then he wouldn't either—a brilliant reframe.

5. *Hopes and revelations.* Jesus asked a blind man, "What do you want me to do for you?" (Mk 10:51). The man longed to see, and Jesus granted his desire. But Jesus also asked the same question just a few verses earlier of his own disciples James and John (Mk 10:36). Instead of healing and restoration, they asked for glory and a position of honor to sit on Jesus' right and left in his glory. It angered the other disciples and launched Jesus into a significant teaching moment about his approach to power and authority. The same question revealed different motives, which wielded different effects. Jesus asked because he wanted others to verbalize what they truly longed for, to reveal the most important matters of the heart.

6. *Modeling the heart of the Father.* Jesus operates in perfect unity within the Trinity with God the Father and the Holy Spirit. Jesus said he only does what he sees his Father doing (Jn 5:19-20). Jesus' questions reflect the heart of his Father: creating opportunities for relationship while communicating both the accessibility and the mystery of God himself, the God who wants to be known by his creation and yet who cannot be fully known. Jesus simply did what he saw modeled. He still does.

WHERE DID JESUS LEARN TO ASK GREAT QUESTIONS?

If questions were so central to his life, where did he learn to ask them? Jesus' cultural and educational context shaped much of his understanding of questions and his use of them. The Jewishness of Jesus cannot be over-emphasized, especially as it relates to his education.

Theological discussion saturated with questions was not the exception; it was the expectation. Jews believe that the Torah urges children to ask questions about God (Ex 12:26-27; 13:14; Deut 6:20-21). Questions are a foundational element of Jewish parenting and education; teaching children to ask questions is *a religious duty*. To be Jewish *is* to ask questions. But it is also essential for Jewish parents to teach their children that not every question has an immediate and understandable answer. Uncertainty and mystery amid questions is not only acceptable; it is required.

Even today, the highest praise for students in yeshiva, a school that studies Torah, is reserved not for those who answer correctly but for those who ask perceptively. Back to twelve-year-old Jesus in the temple: the religious leaders were amazed by his questions and his understanding (Lk 2:36-47). The Talmud, a central text of Judaism, contains a number of rabbinic discussions pertaining to Jewish law, ethics, customs, and history. But it's also full of hundreds of pages of debates sparked by questions. One can only imagine how this might form the minds and hearts of young Jews. It certainly shaped Jesus.

In the Gospels Jesus was called rabbi, and a good rabbi knows how to ask great questions. On numerous occasions Jesus was asked a question, but he rarely answered it—he would just ask another question.

A lawyer tested him: "Teacher, what must I do to inherit eternal life?" Jesus asked right back, "What is written in the Law? How do you read it?" (Lk 10:25-26).

The religious leaders asked, "Is it right to pay the imperial tax to Caesar or not?" He requested a coin and asked, "Whose image is this?" (Mt 22:17-22).

Some Pharisees tested him: "Is it lawful for a man to divorce his wife?" Jesus' response: "What did Moses command you?" (Mk 10:2-3).

Did Jesus not know the answers? Was he dodging the question? Why was he being so difficult? For those of us in the West, this dynamic can be confusing and sometimes frustrating. It might be less accurate to claim Jesus conducted Q&A sessions and more accurate to state he often held Q&Q sessions. But if we look carefully under the hood, we can understand what's going on in the story: Jesus actually *does* answer the question; the answer is often *inside of the question*. In our Western mindset, when we're asked a question ("What is two plus two?") we offer a clear answer ("Four"). In a rabbinic understanding, we would answer a question ("What is two plus two?") by asking another question ("What is sixteen divided by four?"). If we have eyes to see it, the responsive question *is* the answer—or hints toward it.

HOW MANY DID HE ASK?

About 15 percent of the sentences in the New Testament end in question marks. That's around *one thousand questions* found in the Greek New Testament, with about six hundred found in the Gospels, most notably in John and Matthew.

How many questions did Jesus ask in the New Testament? I've seen claims ranging from 305 to 339, of which the most common number cited is 307. But in my own study I found more. Using the New International Version, I counted 297 direct questions of Jesus in the Gospels. However, Jesus also posed twenty-seven indirect questions through characters and figures embedded in his parables as a way to advance the plot of those stories. These twenty-seven questions are used as a rhetorical device to keep the listener's attention. Additionally, many people miss (although it's easy to spot in a red-letter-edition Bible) that Jesus asks a question in the book of Acts: "Saul, Saul, why do you persecute me?" (Acts 9:4). Adding it all up, I've identified a total of 325 questions.

Yet despite my research, these numbers are still not *entirely* accurate. Due to nuanced language in translation and no punctuation in the original text, it is impossible to know *exactly* how many questions appear in the Bible. Some questions may be understood more as

statements and some statements as questions. In some overlapping
stories in the Gospels, one author records Jesus' words as a question
while another records it as a statement.

Nonetheless, we can confidently say there are over three hundred
recorded questions of Jesus in the Bible. Catch this: he was *almost forty
times more likely to ask a question than he was to give a direct answer.* Do
you find it a bit unsettling that if you met Jesus on the street, he would
have more likely asked you a question than given you an answer?

While Jesus asked a lot of questions in the Gospels, it's also important to note just how many people asked *him* questions. Some have
claimed that Jesus was asked 183 questions. Again, we're unable to have
complete confidence in the exact number of questions Jesus was asked
due to cultural nuances in translation. But after studying the questions
in the Gospels, if I had to offer my best answer, I would land at 187. Also,
what I find fascinating—even a bit perplexing—is that *Jesus only answered five questions directly and four other questions semidirectly.* (I've
included the list of these direct and semidirect answers in Resource 4
in the back of the book.) By that count, Jesus either ignored, deflected,
redirected, or indirectly answered 178 questions. Regardless of the
exact number, we can be sure of this: *Jesus chose to directly answer an
astonishingly small percentage of the questions he was asked.*

THE CONTEXT OF JESUS' QUESTIONS

The power of Jesus' questions in the Gospels makes more sense when we
understand the context in which he asked them—the audience, the
location, and what prompted the question in the first place. Two of my
favorite examples are worth unpacking a bit here.

Jesus and his disciples traveled to the little fishing village of Bethsaida, where people brought him a blind man and begged Jesus to heal
him. Jesus led the blind man outside of the village, spat on his eyes, and
asked, "Do you see anything?" The man responded, "I see people; they
look like trees walking around" (Mk 8:22-26). Why was the man's

vision less than clear? Did Jesus make a mistake? Mark does not offer an explicit response other than to mention that Jesus put his hands on the man's eyes a second time and fully restored his sight. Curiously, Jesus sent the man back to his home village and told him not to tell anyone. The details are a bit puzzling. Why did Jesus lead the blind man *outside* of the village, away from others? Why did he not restore his sight in the presence of the man's neighbors, in hopes they might also believe? Why did he appear to conduct a two-part healing? And why did he command him to remain silent about the matter?

What I failed to notice until recently is that we're unable to fully interpret this story without seeing the connection to the one preceding it. Previously, the disciples had neglected to bring the leftover bread on the boat after Jesus fed the four thousand. Jesus cautioned them to be on guard against the yeast of the Pharisees and Herod. Not understanding what he was saying, the disciples believed Jesus was referencing their forgetfulness about the bread (Mk 8:15-16). Seeing that they still didn't have a clue, Jesus unleashed six successive questions, including, "Do you have eyes but fail to see . . . ?" (Mk 8:18). After some discussion, he concluded with a scathing rhetorical question: "Do you still not understand?" (Mk 8:21). Jesus and the disciples then traveled to Bethsaida, where the townspeople asked Jesus to heal the blind man.

Are the dots connecting for you? Jesus did not primarily intend to teach the blind man an important lesson. Instead, he intended to teach his disciples, who had not understood, *that they were the ones who had eyes but could not see.* True, the blind man received his sight (a tremendous gift, no doubt), but the disciples received a crucial lesson about sight that arrives through their faith, not their retinas. After healing the blind man, Jesus might have implied a silent question: "*Now* do you understand?" By understanding the location of his questions and by seeing these stories in the larger context, we begin to appreciate the brilliance of Jesus' questions rather than seeing them as mere standalones.

THE MOST IMPORTANT QUESTION IN THE GOSPELS

Here's a second example. If we understand how the Gospel of Mark is structured, we can grasp the most significant question in the book. The first half of Mark highlights Jesus' emphasis on offering life, while the second half emphasizes the experience of suffering and death. The halfway point of the Gospel is found at the end of chapter eight with Peter's confession that Jesus is the Christ. Peter's statement is the hinge on which the door of the book swings: "You are the Messiah" (Mk 8:29). Up until that point, Jesus' message was about life; immediately after Peter's confession, Jesus predicted his own death and spoke openly and frequently about suffering (Mk 8:31-33).

Jesus and his disciples were traveling to the villages around Caesarea Philippi, which stood in stark contrast to the customs and cultures of Jerusalem. Jerusalem was the geographical and spiritual center of Jewish life, with the massive temple and a pervasive monotheistic belief system among the Jewish people. But Caesarea Philippi, located in the northern region of Israel, flourished as the center of pagan worship. There is a large rock escarpment where dozens of idols are carved into niches, which pay homage to various gods and goddesses. You can visit its location and see them even today. It was on the way to Caesarea Philippi that Jesus asked his disciples, "Who do people say I am?" (Mk 8:27). He wasn't merely taking a personal opinion poll. After their response, he tightened the screws: "But what about you? Who do you say I am?" (Mk 8:29). It was the most personal Level Four question he could ask his disciples. Bump, set, spike.

Jesus could have asked these three questions when he and the disciples were walking the streets of Jerusalem or worshiping in the temple. Could it be that Jesus intentionally waited to ask these questions when they were in a decidedly polytheistic context to ensure his question had more teeth and could evoke the most honest thought? *What, who,* and *how* matter when asking questions, but *where* matters too.

THE TYPES OF QUESTIONS JESUS ASKED

Think of the different types of questions Jesus asked: original, practical, personal, rhetorical, stimulating, hyperbolic, definitive, silencing, clear, and brief questions. But more generally speaking, Conrad Gempf's book *Jesus Asked* organizes Jesus' questions into five primary categories.

Rebuking questions. They were almost entirely rhetorical in nature. Jesus' most common rebuking question, always directed at the religious experts and teachers of the law, began with "Have you not read . . . ?" Of course they had—but they weren't *living* what they had read. When Peter asked if Jesus could explain his parable, Jesus asked, "Are you still so dull?" (Mt 15:16). When making a point that his disciples were slow to understand, he asked, "Do you still not understand?" (Mk 8:21). If you listen closely, you can hear the exasperation in his voice.

Ordinary, or direct, questions. Sometimes he asked questions primarily for informational and contextual purposes. At the feeding of the five thousand: "How many loaves do you have?" (Mk 6:38). And one of my all-time favorites of Jesus, when he appeared to his disciples after the resurrection: "Do you have anything here to eat?" to which he was handed a piece of broiled fish and ate it (Lk 24:41-42).

Absurd questions. Jesus asked questions to which the answers could not be more obvious. His use of exaggeration and hyperbole disarmed and at times evoked a smile or laughter. "Why do you look at the speck of sawdust in your brother's eye and pay no attention to the plank in your own eye?" (Mt 7:3). A log hanging out of someone's eye . . . *really*? "If your son asks for bread, will [you] give him a stone? Or if he asks for a fish, will [you] give him a snake?" (Mt 7:9-11). Of course not.

Incisive questions. These questions cut right to the heart of the issue and created the richest conditions for transformation to occur. Like a skilled surgeon with a scalpel in hand, Jesus worked on people's hearts with his questions. Oftentimes, they were so personal they drew blood—not to cause hurt or harm, but to bring about healing and wholeness. One of the most incisive communication tools Jesus utilized was the "how much more" technique, like when he addressed the topic of worry in the Sermon on the Mount. This technique is called a fortiori (Latin for "from the stronger argument"). Jesus placed something over another in an exaggerated comparison to illustrate a stark contrast. *If these seemingly small things are taken care of by God, how much more will he take care of us?*

Response-oriented questions. With these, Jesus expected to receive a response. He asked the woman at the well, "Will you give me a drink?" (Jn 4:7). But even these response-oriented questions are an invitation for formation. The first question in the Gospel of John is, "What do you want?" (Jn 1:38). Placing this at the beginning forces us to ask ourselves, *What is it that I'm seeking?*

Jesus was brilliant when it came to asking questions. His questions weren't primarily for information but for incision; they were not to evoke easy answers but to ask difficult, necessary questions, probing the human heart to effectively arrive at what truly matters.

As Christians, we study Jesus' teachings. We study his miracles. We study his parables. But seldom do we ever study his questions—what he asked, where he asked, how he asked them—and ultimately the impact those questions had on people's lives. I can't help but notice how often his questions led and continue to lead to awareness, growth, and transformation. If we're serious about wanting Jesus to be our Master Teacher, we should also be learning from not just his answers but also his questions.

And who better to learn how to ask better questions from than Jesus?

THE QUESTIONS WE ASK GOD

What's behind our desire
to inquire of the Creator?

How long, O Lord?

King David (Ps 13:1 ESV)

My God, my God, why have you forsaken me?

Jesus (Mt 27:46)

WE MIGHT FEEL SOME LEVEL OF COMFORT asking questions of others, but what about asking questions of God? Many of us may feel skittish. *Who am I to question God? Would it make any difference? Would doing so reveal a weak faith?* The Scriptures are filled with people who asked God questions. Jesus himself asked bold, direct questions of his Father.

Several years ago, I decided to conduct an audit of the questions I ask God. I realized that in the earlier years of my faith journey, I rarely asked him questions. I just told him what I thought—statements, requests, complaints, gratitude, concerns. All good things. But one of the greatest changes in my prayer life has been how many questions I now ask God when I pray and how frequently I ask them. They are honest, intense, and raw. *Why haven't you healed my friend who's courageously battling cancer? Why, God, are you hiding from me? Will things ever change?* Paradoxically, my questions of God have bolstered my faith, helping me to draw closer to him and feel more connected.

A. W. Tozer has a striking opening line in his book *The Knowledge of the Holy*: "What comes into our minds when we think about God is the most important thing about us." I remember reading that line in my college dorm room. It touched something deep within me. *What do I think about God?* I wondered. *And how does that affect how I go about each day?* If Tozer's statement is true, then the questions we ask about God are essential to what comes into our mind.

One question I love to ask others, old and young, is: *If you could ask God two or three questions and he had to answer, what would you ask?* It gives me a glimpse into what really matters to others. The power of a question lies in the fact that it reveals our true desires. The types of questions we ask God can give us a glimpse into what we think about him—and nothing is more clarifying than what we ask when we experience failure, suffering, and hardship. *What do we do when we are laid bare under the weight of suffering and pain? What do we assume about the world and the God who made it when we meet our limitations and feel the hardships that life often brings our way?*

Most frequently, the questions come in the form of why. *Why did this happen? Why me? Why them?* often followed by *Where were you, God?* Taking time to listen carefully will reveal our truest, deepest desires. God asked questions, and he created and wired us to ask questions. So when we ask questions, what if we are living out what God intended us to do? What if God *invites us* and *encourages us* to ask him questions, even if they might make others blush?

THE QUESTIONS OF CHILDREN

What can children teach us about how to ask God questions?

My friend Kelly was nearing the end of a grueling journey through her PhD program, trying to juggle her studies and her job while raising three young kids with her husband, Brad. After four solid days of writing her comprehensive exams, she'd barely seen her kids. As she was tucking them into bed, her eight-year-old son Max asked, "Mom, do you feel brave because you had something hard to do and you did it anyway?"

Trying to hold back tears she replied, "Yes, Max, I do feel brave."

She suddenly realized that amid all her fears about how continuing her education may have negatively impacted her kids, she hadn't considered the ways that watching her pursue her degree would positively influence them. What a beautiful question from a child: *Do you feel brave?*

Warren Berger believes that the master questioners in our world today are a typical four-year-old girl. Jesus asserted that unless we change and become like little children, we will never enter the kingdom of heaven (Mt 18:3). They freely, naturally, and unapologetically inquire about seemingly everything. *Might there be a connection between Jesus' statement about becoming more childlike and asking questions?* Questions help us to see things with new eyes, and children do that best. Could Jesus be saying that if we are to enter the kingdom of heaven, we must possess the humility and wonder of a child?

What if childlike faith is revealed in the quality and the quantity of the questions we ask—including the questions we ask our Father? As the seventeenth-century English philosopher John Locke wrote, "I think there is frequently more to be learn'd from the unexpected questions of a child than the discourses of men." Try asking a roomful of children, "What is God like?" and you'll be enlightened, entertained, and amazed all at once. Children teach us that God wants us to ask him more honest questions than what we're currently asking.

LIQUID TEARS

Let's talk about theobiology for a moment. It's the term I use to describe when we're exploring and appreciating God by noticing the numerous intricate ways he created and designed our physical bodies. For example, isn't it amazing that when we cry God did not design our bodies to leak water out of our elbows or the big toe on our right foot? When we are moved to tears—out of beauty, fear, pain, joy, loneliness, or suffering—we shed tears out of our eyes, the window to our soul.

If God designed us to leak water out of our elbow or big toe, we might have a soaked shirt or a wet sock, but we would be able to hide it fairly easily. But it's much harder to hide our faces when our eyes are red and our cheeks are soaked with warm tears. When we cry, God has uniquely and intentionally designed our bodies to send physical signals to others and ourselves that say, *Please pay attention. Something significant and sacred is happening to me right now, and I need to know I am not alone. I need to be seen in this moment.* Have you ever thanked God for such a thoughtful design of your body?

One of the best ways to pay attention in these moments is to ask ourselves questions. *God, what do I need to pay attention to right now? What's happening in my soul in this moment? Why am I moved so deeply?* Frederick Buechner writes,

> Whenever you find tears in your eyes, especially unexpected tears, it is well to pay the closest attention. They are not only telling you something about the secret of who you are, but more often than not God is speaking to you through them of the mystery of where you have come from and is summoning you to where, if your soul is to be saved, you should go to next.

This compassionate theobiological design of our bodies is God's gift to the world and to us. He's created us as relational beings, creatures who need each other, especially in hardship and suffering. We often don't see this as a gift. In fact, one of our most common responses when we have tears in our eyes, especially as men, is to offer an apology. "I'm sorry," we mutter as we quickly wipe away the wet. When others have apologized in these sacred moments, I gently smile and assure them that they don't need to apologize for their tears. I remind them that this is a significant and sacred moment worthy of reflection, and I am grateful they trust me with it.

If we can override our culturally conditioned impulse to apologize for our tears and instead ask why they are there in the first place, we will be wiser for it. And if we can gently and carefully help others ask themselves why their tears are present, it can be a beautiful act of hospitality. One of the most tangible ways to express love and extend grace is to see others in their tears and move toward them in gentle, attentive compassion.

Several years ago, Steve, a reporter at our local newspaper, reached out saying he'd like to do a feature story on our church about an initiative we were launching to bless the community. Steve asked if he could meet with me to ask a few questions and arrange a visit to our church. I agreed to meet on one condition: after the story was published, I would treat him to lunch and ask him questions about what he experienced interacting with our people. He said that in all his years of reporting nobody had ever made that request, but he obliged.

After the piece was published, Steve and I met for lunch at a diner a few blocks from my home. As we sat down, he told me he wasn't a very religious person and didn't want to talk much about faith during our conversation. I told him that was completely fine by me. To get to know him, I asked a few introductory questions—How did you first get into journalism? What do you like about your job?—Level One- and Two-type questions.

And then I asked what I thought was another simple, get-to-know-you type of question: "Tell me your story. Who is Steve?" I had hardly finished asking the question when he began to cry. It was slightly awkward as he stared down at the table, but he kept going. I sensed he needed to share some things that he'd been wanting to express to someone who would listen. The more he talked, the more intensely the tears began to flow. He poured out his story. His insecurities and doubts. His broken dreams. A marriage headed for divorce. A job in which he found little fulfillment. The angsty feeling of wondering

where his life was headed. After a few moments, the waitress swung by
to check on us, only to see Steve in a puddle of tears. Caught off guard
and unsure what to do, she backed away slowly and muttered, "I'll leave
you two alone and come back in a few minutes." In our cultural dis-ease
with tears and grief, her response didn't come as a surprise.

Trying to pay attention to what might be stirring below the surface,
I took a risk and tried to move to the next level. "Tears are essentially
liquid prayers," I said. "I know you said you're not really a religious
person. But can you put words to the prayers that your face is praying
right now?" At this point Steve began to shake as he wept. After a long
silence, he collected himself and said, "Right now my face is praying,
'God, help me. I'm alone. I just want to know I am not going to be
alone and I'm going to be okay. Help me . . . just help me . . . just help
me.'" The simplicity, honesty, and the courage by which Steve shared
was moving.

When I'm with people who cry, I think about Buechner and the
liquid-prayers question—and when it's appropriate, I'll ask it. It often
leads to amazingly rich conversations, most especially with those who
describe themselves as not being very religious. I'm so grateful that
God, in our most vulnerable and significant moments, designed liquid
to leak out of the most relational part of our body.

FAILURE, HARDSHIP, AND SUFFERING:
A FORMATIVE TIME FOR HONEST QUESTIONS

The Psalms have been the prayer book of the church for centuries, and
over the past handful of years it has become the book I frequent the
most. Numerous questions abound in these written prayers. Some are
rhetorical, uplifting, and full of praise.

"The LORD is my light and my salvation—whom shall I fear? The
LORD is the stronghold of my life—of whom shall I be afraid?" (Ps 27:1).

"What shall I return to the LORD for all his goodness to me?"
(Ps 116:12).

"If you, LORD, kept a record of sins, Lord, who could stand?" (Ps 130:3).

And yet the Psalms, these inspired words of God, contain a startlingly large number of prayers that would have been labeled R-rated by the film industry. There are intense accusations against God that he has not done his job and has abandoned his people. Praying that God would pour out wrath on their enemies? For people to seize their infants and bash them against the rocks (Ps 137:9)? These brash, direct, in-your-face psalms contain intense emotion—and some buck-naked honest questions that often include *How long? When?* and *Why?*

"How long, O LORD? Will you forget me forever? How long will you hide your face from me?" (Ps 13:1 ESV).

"Why are you so far from saving me, from the words of my groaning?" (Ps 22:1 ESV).

"Why, LORD, do you reject me and hide your face from me?" (Ps 88:14).

These come out of a place of immense disorientation, hurt, and abandonment. These types of prayers are called psalms of lament. Some of them are so bold and extreme, involving such unhinged emotional outbursts, it makes me wonder whether, if the psalmist wrote these today, he would ever be hired at a church. What's startling is that the Israelites didn't just pray these intense questions—they *sang* them. Yet what I find equally startling and comforting is that David, who penned many of these questions, was called *a man after God's own heart* (Acts 13:22).

There is a surprisingly large amount of lament in the Bible even outside of the Psalms. An entire book is named after it, penned by Jeremiah: the book of Lamentations. A large section of the Old Testament books of Job, Isaiah, Jeremiah, and many of the minor Prophets are saturated with lament. In fact, approximately one-third of the Psalms are labeled as psalms of lament. Lament realizes that pain is a terrible thing to waste and gives us permission to grieve, to go through the mess and not around it. And yet, when was the last time you sang a lament song based on Scripture in a worship service? *Why does it feel so strange and out of place, offensive even, to ask God intense, in-your-face-type questions when there are so many throughout Scripture?* We are often reluctant to express lament because it feels as though we're just complaining, throwing a temper tantrum before God. It's uncomfortable and angsty. Messy and emotional.

The Psalms often make us squirm because they bring up such difficult and complex questions birthed out of complex emotions. What makes these questions so uncomfortable is that while they are voiced freely, they are most often left unanswered. Lament can seem brazenly disrespectful. Who would talk to a person in authority or a loved one like that, let alone the Creator of the universe? When we are walking, limping, crawling, dragging—or being dragged—through the valley of the shadow of death, there is no energy to pray nice and polite prayers. Mourning takes practice. And this is why we need psalms of lament.

"There's so much for us to be thankful for," one friend told me as we talked about lament over coffee. "Can't we just move on and think about positive things?" Some believe laments are a crutch, or even a sign of spiritual immaturity. But it's the opposite. A lament is soaking wet with faith: a rare, pure form of faith that longs for God to keep his word. As Holocaust survivor Elie Wiesel wrote, "I have not lost faith in God. I have moments of anger and protest. Sometimes I've been closer to him for that reason." In times of lament—when we feel disappointment, abandonment, disorientation, and pain—it's good to ask three questions: *What do I want? What do I miss? What do I need?*

There is a three-part structure that holds for almost all the psalms of lament: a complaint, a petition, and a resolution. In Psalm 13, we see a complaint in the first two verses. Then there is a petition in verses 3-4. The lament psalms experience a "turn"—turning away from our honest questions of ourselves toward the goodness and faithfulness of God, even in the midst of pain. That resolution shows up in verses 5-6, the final two verses in the psalm.

QUESTIONS TO ASK IN TIMES OF LAMENT

What do I want?

What do I miss?

What do I need?

How did I walk into this room? What sorrow/joy did I bring with me?

Why am I here?

What am I truly feeling?

What has this situation taken away from me? What has it not taken away from me? What has it given to me?

What do I need to lament honestly and courageously in this season?

Despite all the pain and suffering, what is God doing in and through me right now? What might he want to do?

The heading to Psalm 70 in the New English Translation reads, "For the music director, by David; written to get God's attention." I love that. *God, I'm talking to you. I need to know you're listening.* I've found that the more pain, suffering, and abandonment I feel, the more honest my questions. I find it both startling and immensely comforting to know that God wasn't scared away, turned off, or offended by the brashness of David's R-rated questions. Nor is he with mine or yours. Because of this, I have permission to pray as honestly as I can muster. This is one of the reasons why I love reading the Psalms. It's also a reason why I love writing my own psalms of lament. God gives us clear permission to ask him questions, without apology, to help us express and emote as intensely as we desire in order to connect with him. What a gift.

The power of a good question is that it often reveals our true desires—and nobody more than God loves to know what we truly desire. He not only allows us to ask him questions but strongly encourages it.

What if the issue isn't that we're asking God honest and direct questions but that we're not asking enough of them?

PART 3

BECOMING A PERSON OF QUESTION-ABLE INFLUENCE

Have you ever been around leaders who only offer answers, utter opinions, and give orders?

What about leaders who humbly, thoughtfully, and courageously ask questions?

Which type of leader is easier to follow?

How would you rate your ability to ask great questions?

How would those you lead rate your ability to ask great questions?

What questions continually guide your life as a leader?

Have you ever asked yourself, Why do I have the right to lead? Why am I convinced others should follow me?

It has been said that questions develop leaders, but would it not also be true that leaders continually develop questions?

What does it say about a leader who doesn't ask questions?

What if the role of the leader of the future isn't primarily about giving answers?

What if the paradigm of the leader-as-expert is replaced with the leader-as-lead-questioner?

When leading others, what might questions provide that answers simply cannot?

QUESTIONS AS INFLUENCE

What if the best leaders aren't those
who know the right answers but are instead
those who ask the right questions?

*The number one difference between a Nobel Prize winner
and others is not IQ or work ethic, but
that they ask bigger questions.*

PETER DRUCKER

*You can tell whether a man is clever by his answers.
You can tell whether a man is wise by his questions.*

NAGUIB MAHFOUZ

AFTER GRADUATING FROM the United States Naval
Academy in 1946, Jimmy applied for the government's presti-
gious nuclear submarine program. The program was led by the ever-
demanding Admiral Hyman Rickover. During his interview, Rickover
told Jimmy he could discuss any topics he wished to talk about with
him. The young graduate was well-versed in current events, seamanship,
music, literature, naval tactics, and marksmanship, to name a few. But
Rickover grilled him. The more questions Jimmy was asked, the more
he realized he was in over his head.

Finally, the young officer heard the question he was waiting for, the one he could use to redeem himself. Admiral Rickover asked, "How did you stand in your graduating class at the Naval Academy?"

"I graduated fifty-ninth in my class of 820, sir," he replied confidently. He was sure he would be congratulated, but the Admiral was not impressed. Then came another question: "Did you do your best?"

He was tempted to quickly answer yes. But the more he thought of his time at the Naval Academy, the more he realized when he could have learned more, applied himself more, and prepared himself to learn about enemies and allies, strategies, and weapons.

He cleared his throat and responded, "No sir, I did not always do my best."

Admiral Rickover then turned around in his chair and promptly ended the interview by asking a final question: "And why not?"

That question haunted and motivated Jimmy for the rest of his life, shaping him in ways that eventually led him to be the US president and Nobel Prize winner we know as Jimmy Carter.

GADFLIES AND DELIVERING BABIES

If you had to pick one person in history who was known for asking questions, it very well might be Socrates. An early Greek philosopher and teacher who lived more than twenty-four hundred years ago, he believed that disciplined and rigorous questioning was the most effective way to learn. Socrates, famous as he was, never wrote down a single word of his teachings. Fortunately, his student Plato did. Through his questions, Socrates relentlessly challenged the deep-seated and previously unquestioned customs of the day. He questioned the assumptions of his students and forced them to consider new perspectives. The citizens of Athens became incensed. Three young men, Anytus, Meletus, and Lycon, brought legal proceedings against the seventy-one-year-old and charged him with corrupting and poisoning the minds of the youth of Athens. Socrates was sentenced to death by drinking hemlock. His questions were so unsettling and disruptive he was killed for them. Despite his tragic end, the Socratic method—question-oriented dialogue, exploration, and learning—became his greatest contribution to Western thinking.

Socrates described questions with two metaphors. The first is a gadfly, which bites and irritates livestock and other animals. Questions serve a similar purpose; they can sting or irritate to the point that they cannot be ignored. A good question provokes us to think, feel, and act differently. Admiral Rickover's question certainly stung young Jimmy Carter and got his attention.

But Socrates's second metaphor is even more impactful: a midwife. His father was a stonecutter and sculptor, and his mother was a midwife. He believed that someone who asked thoughtful questions assisted others in bringing new life into the world. Interestingly, the word midwife in Greek (*maieutikos*) is where we get the English word *maieutic*, an adjective describing someone who asks questions to draw out a response from others. A maieutic posture is akin to a midwife assisting mothers in delivery—a painful, messy, yet sacred time of ushering in new life. Socrates stated, "My art of midwifery is in general like theirs; the only difference is that my patients are men, not women, and my concern is not with the body but with the soul that is in travail at birth."

Several years ago when I first learned this metaphor, it grabbed me by the throat and didn't let go. I was so intrigued I sought out a friend who is a midwife and asked her about her vocation. I knew, of course, that her ultimate role was to assist mothers in labor and delivery. But I asked, from her perspective, what she *actually* did in those significant situations. What specifically was her posture and relationship with an expectant mother? What was she thinking and feeling at the moment a human life came into the world? "My role," she said, "is to hold sacred space for God to bring about new life." Her response helped me to understand, quite possibly for the first time, the power and potential of great questions.

The modern English word for midwife has a Middle English origin: *mit wif*, quite literally, "with-woman." The midwife receives her cues from and always depends on the work of the delivering mother. Midwives don't usher new life into the world; instead, they facilitate, support, and assist in the midst of it. Like midwives, great questions open doors and release nurturers.

Building on Socrates's midwife imagery, Bill Easum and Tom Bandy describe faith leaders as spiritual midwives. Instead of leaders seeing themselves as mothers giving birth to their own ideas and dreams, Easum and Bandy suggest a shift in posture: instead, faith leaders support other mothers as they give birth to the ideas and dreams God has given to them. Question-oriented leaders enable others to give birth to what resides inside of them; they provide the support, encouragement, guidance, perspective, and framework by asking questions in the process.

When someone I've just met asks what I do, I often respond by saying I'm a spiritual midwife. I get some interesting looks, but I'm almost always asked follow-up questions that lead to fascinating conversations. The irony of this metaphor is not lost on me: not only am I a male, but I'm also the father of two adopted sons, which means my wife and I have never experienced labor and delivery firsthand. Yet I find the image of a midwife to be the most striking and meaningful metaphor I've encountered.

If we are to think like midwives we have to release our agendas, which is why listening and asking questions feels unnatural and, at times, scary. If a midwife sought to control the situation, she would run the real risk of stifling the role she's called to maintain in the process. Just as a midwife must listen well and take her cues from the mother while also shaping the environment, leaders must do the same. Shaping, however, is not the same thing as controlling. Midwives are attendants to the birthing process. The delicate work of a midwife requires an openness to enter fully into a situation without dominating it. The midwife must possess the confidence to help and assist, but also the humility to get out of the way and realize the story is not primarily centered on her.

BUILDING TRUST, BEARING PAIN, BRINGING HOPE

At the foundational level, a leader is someone who builds trust, bears pain, and brings hope. A leader is not determined by title, charisma, education, or position but by posture and mindset. True leadership is always and only built on the foundation of trust. We are in an age of a large amount of information and a small amount of trust. But without trust, leadership is bankrupt. Trust is built on thick bonds of relationship, and great questions build trust. I live by the strong conviction that leaders should be the most curious people on the planet. If we want information, we can Google it. But if what we're after is clarity and connection, we need questions. Our world isn't in need of more leaders who are smarter, more eloquent, and more efficient; instead, we need more leaders who are wiser, humbler, and more curious.

Jesus had a few things to say about leadership. In Matthew 20, Jesus completely disrupts the assumption that leadership is about wielding power over others. He taught that leadership does not come by coercion, intimidation, or manipulation. Authority is not to be used to lord over people; instead, it should compel us to serve others (Mt 20:20-28). And asking thoughtful, caring questions is a meaningful form of service.

One of the most formative questions I've ever been asked regarding leadership came in my twenties. I'll never forget the day I sat with my mentor, Tom, talking about servant leadership in John 13 as we ate burritos at Chipotle. He asked me something that has stayed with me through the years: *"Is it better to be a servant who leads or a leader who serves?"*

It's not semantics, he told me; the answer has significant implications, especially as people of faith. If you assume the posture of a leader who serves, and then you're taken out of a leadership position, it will mess with your identity significantly. But if you assume the posture of a servant who leads, and then you're taken out of a leadership position, it will change what you do day to day, but it doesn't have to change your identity. It's better to be a servant who leads. Few things have shaped my philosophy of leadership more as a faith leader than Tom's question.

LEADERSHIFT

The late leadership and organizational expert Peter Drucker said, "The leader of the past may have been the person who knew how to tell, but certainly the leader of the future will be the person who knows how to ask." Leaders who shape the future will be those who shift from a mindset of leader-as-answer-giver to leader-as-lead-question-asker. When we possess a posture of question-asking, we have the opportunity to reach into people's souls and truly connect with them. Those who refuse to make this shift will become increasingly irrelevant, but those who are able to will hold the keys to the future.

What if leadership has more to do with starting conversations than ending them? What would be the result if leaders were known more for their questions than their answers?

QUESTION-ABLE INFLUENCE

Leadership is difficult; sometimes it can be excruciating. Our world is so desperate for healthy leadership precisely *because* it's so hard. It's a lifelong journey of learning to steward this mysterious and sometimes exhausting gift in the direction of a purpose greater than ourselves. What makes leadership even more difficult is that the hardest person you will ever lead will always be yourself.

Which means as leaders we must ask others questions, but we must also ask *ourselves* the most direct and incisive questions of all. Justin Irving and Mark Strauss studied hundreds of Christian leaders, looking for patterns and themes. They found the most effective leaders were those who spent time in frequent reflection and asked themselves the important questions *first* before asking others:

> The presence of leaders who honestly evaluate themselves before seeking to evaluate others was a statistically significant predictor of effective leadership practices. In fact, *this self-leadership practice had the most dominant predictive effect on leadership effectiveness out of all the leadership practices studied.* (emphasis mine)

Show me a healthy, centered, fruitful leader, and I'll show you someone who has engaged in intentional reflection prompted by significant questions.

GOOD QUESTIONS LEADERS CAN ASK THEMSELVES

What gives me the right to lead others?

How can I deepen trust with my team?

How can I serve them in such a way that they know to their core that I value who they are more than what they contribute to our organization?

What does my team need from me that will help them thrive?

For others to flourish, where do I need to be more involved, and where do I need to get out of the way?

Because I have power and authority, who, in turn, is now flourishing because of it?

Am I embracing the posture of a humble servant as I lead others? How would I know for sure?

How might we grow in our question-able influence?

LEADERS AS CURIOUS AMPLIFIERS

What's the difference between good leaders and great leaders? Developmental coach and author Jennifer Garvey Berger studied this question, and her research found two significant differences: amplification and curiosity.

Great leaders amplify others. They help others to succeed and reach their goals. They are quick to praise and celebrate others for their hard work and contributions. They focus on others and not on themselves. They are Amplifiers. This sounds quite similar to David Brooks's concept mentioned earlier about people being either Illuminators or Diminishers. Leaders amplify others by asking themselves questions like, *Am I investing in the success* of *others? Do people elevate when they are in the gravitational pull of my life?*

Great leaders are also curious. They tend to listen to the whispers around them to know if something significant is going on. It doesn't mean they believe all the whispers, but they are at least aware of what is being said. They pick up on little signals that make a big difference.

Amplification and curiosity are symbiotic and synergistic. The more curious leaders are about others, the more people feel amplified. And amplifying others stokes leaders' curiosity even more. Great leaders are curious Amplifiers with their arrows pointing out toward others, continually asking questions.

People who ask courageous, compassionate, curious questions— people who live as curious Amplifiers—are worthy of being followed. And a person who is being followed is called a leader.

QUESTION-ASKING AS FORMATION

How do our questions shape
who we are becoming?

Where have you come from and where are you going?

Genesis 16:8

What do you want?

Jesus (Mk 10:51)

G REAT QUESTIONS can come out of thin air—quite literally. Meghan Good sat next to a young Hindu man on an international flight. During small talk, it came up that Meghan was studying at a seminary. The man was excited, as he had never met a Christian before. As they talked about their respective faiths, he asked her a question that caught her completely off guard: "What *don't* you like about your faith?"

For her, the question didn't compute. She tried to bring sense to his question. *Dislike something about my faith?* she thought. *Am I even allowed to dislike elements of my faith?* With measured vulnerability and sincerity, the young man described various aspects of his own faith and practice that he found unsettling and difficult. Good described her experience this way:

What don't you like about your faith? I had zero answers at the time. Truth be told, I was scandalized by the question. But the longer I thought about it, the more it seemed like it was my total lack of an answer that should really concern me. . . . No single question I have ever been asked has more efficiently propelled me to a new frontier of spiritual growth. With the man's question echoing in my head, I began to notice uncomfortable teachings of Jesus that I had been reading around for years. I began to feel a real sense of friction between Jesus' worldview and my own. I was forced to ask myself seriously for the first time why I was so sure I knew better than him.

No one has ever asked me that question again. But I wish they would. Because boy, do I now have answers. Things I wish Jesus hadn't taught. Parts of my faith that I find painful, frustrating, inconvenient—parts that rub directly against my intuitions about life and the world. I now have a whole list of bones to pick with Jesus. And that's how I know I have a Lord and not an idol.

QUESTION-ASKING AS SPIRITUAL FORMATION

In our frenzied and frenetic world, there may not be a more important time to cultivate our inner life than right now. In the words of psychologist, author, and speaker Larry Crabb, real and lasting change requires us to look inward and ask—and be asked—questions about our inner life. Yet we often envelop ourselves in distractions, surface-level interactions, and highly controlled experiences. We arrange rather than change, and in doing so, we don't become the fully formed person God desires us to be. Regardless of our age, it's important for us to ask, *What kind of old man or woman do I want to be?*

Can you notice the questions you are asking yourself in this season— what you care about, what you hope for, what makes you afraid? What might that reveal about your soul? Dallas Willard was fond of saying that one of the most revelatory questions regarding the state of our souls is to ask, *What's bothering me?* When I'm agitated or angsty or impatient or irritable or downright angry, which happens much more often than I'd like to admit, I've learned to take a step back and ask, *What's going on here? Why am I bothered right now? What do I need to pay attention to currently?*

Some people are tempted to ignore their inner struggle and manage life through the pain as best they can. Or they realize something is wrong and struggle to find their way through life, which Crabb called "shallow copers." They deal with life by handling what they are able to and ignoring all the rest. He named this approach the "managed life," by which people focus on living by a set of principles to be successful. The driving question: *How do I look and feel good?*

Crabb named the second group "troubled reflectors": those who are unable to eliminate that gnawing awareness that something is wrong. They wrestle with the dark and painful elements of life that they are unable to fully address or understand. He called this stage the "wounded life." In this stage, people are driven to do whatever it takes to solve the pain and the problem to return to the managed life. When pain and trouble arise, those in the wounded life ask why ("Why did you do this to me, God? Why did this happen to me?"). Ultimately, the primary driving question is, *What do I need to do to get back to looking and feeling good?*

We experience real and lasting change—true spiritual formation—when we face difficulties with a large dose of reality rather than live in fantasy or hopeful sentimentality. This honest assessment creates hope in us, which leads to deep change. This stage is called the "forming life." The driving question is, *What is God doing in me through this?* In this approach, we focus on releasing the Holy Spirit to do work through our pain rather than ignoring or wallowing in it. Avoiding the tough questions and refusing to confront the difficult issues of life means neglecting a significantly transforming encounter with God. When we ask the right questions, we can steward moments of joy and gratitude as well as life's inevitable experiences of pain and suffering.

A. W. TOZER'S SELF-EXAMINATION QUESTIONS

What do I want the most?

What do I think about the most?

How am I using my money?

What am I doing with my free time?

What company am I keeping?

What and who do I admire?

What am I laughing at?

So what are the kinds of questions you're asking yourself these days? Can you name them? Take a moment to write them down in the margin or in the blank pages at the back of the book. *Do your questions focus more on the container of your life (the managed life and the wounded life) or the contents (the forming life)?* If you want to be spiritually formed to be more like Jesus, one of the best questions you can ask yourself is, *What is God's invitation to me in this situation?*

When you change your questions, you change the trajectory of your own formation.

QUESTIONS AS PRAYER

Have you ever noticed how similar praying and asking questions are? They sometimes feel difficult, yet we know that engaging in them helps us to connect. They require courage because they can be vulnerable and lead us to new terrain. Children oftentimes seem natural at both, but as adults we tend to struggle.

When my prayers are stuck and feel dry, I return to one of my favorite stories in the Gospels: Jesus' interaction with the blind man named Bartimaeus. While walking through the crowd, Jesus heard a blind man call out in desperation, "Jesus, Son of David, have mercy on me!" (Mk 10:47). Jesus stopped, called him over, and asked, "What do you want me to do for you?" (Mk 10:51). On the surface, the snarky side of me reads this and thinks, *I don't know, Jesus, take a wild guess. The man can't see.* But there is something deeper going on here. Jesus knew what Bartimaeus needed, but he wanted Bartimaeus to acknowledge what *he* needed—and to truly understand the implications Jesus' healing might have on his life. Jesus honored Bartimaeus's faith and healed him so that he received sight and followed Jesus along the road (Mk 10:52).

In those seasons when I'm feeling dry and stuck in my prayer life, I imagine Jesus looking at me and asking that same question: *What do you want me to do for you?* Jesus, of course, is not a genie in a bottle who, when rubbed correctly, pops out to grant us three divine wishes. Nor is he the kind of Jesus portrayed by so many preachers in three-piece suits and slicked-back hair on late-night religious television. I certainly am not promoting a "name it and claim it" kind of prosperity gospel here. But I do know God is a loving Father who takes immense delight in hearing what's on his children's hearts. Just as I relish when my sons ask me for something, God takes great joy in hearing what's on our hearts.

When I imagine Jesus asking me that question, sometimes the answer arrives immediately. Peace in a time of uncertainty. Healing from sickness. A colleague to stop annoying me so much. Yet there have been other times it took me several months to identify and voice a clear response. But whatever my response is, it becomes the avenue by which I can re-engage with God. It usually shifts my spiritual wheels from spinning in the mud to gaining traction and moving toward him. Think for a moment: *If you imagined Jesus asking you, "What do you want me to do for you?" what would you say?* More thoroughly, Paul Miller encourages and challenges us to be pointed, intentional, and specific in our prayers by asking four questions: *What's the situation? How do I feel about it? What am I asking God to do?* and *What is God doing in me in this situation?* These questions help to frame our prayers and put the training wheels on as we learn to ride the bike of faith.

ENGAGING SCRIPTURE THROUGH QUESTIONS

The more I ask questions about faith, the more I am driven to Scripture. And the more I read Scripture, the more questions I have about faith. God's redemptive story unfolds in Scripture and continues to invite us into the ongoing adventure of formation. There was a time when a group of friends from church got together twice a month in people's homes, and we simply read a passage of Scripture aloud and then asked two questions: *What are you hearing from Jesus? What are you going to do about it this week?* The discussion was rich, authentic, and generative. And when we convened again, the first question was, *Did you do what you said you were going to do about what you heard from Jesus?* Simple but formative.

There are other ways I engage questions to be formed by Scripture, some by myself and others in group settings. It's tempting to simply look for the answers the Bible gives, but we often neglect to listen for the questions it asks. The most accessible way to begin to do this is to engage with the questions Jesus asked, specifically those found in the Gospel of John. What I love about this particular Gospel is how intentional John was in highlighting and recording Jesus' questions. He frames them in a way that makes the questions of Jesus more personal, as if Jesus is asking us the same questions. His questions are brilliant.

- *"What do you want?"* (Literal translation: *"What are you seeking?"* [Jn 1:38 ESV])
- *"Do you want to get well?"* (Jn 5:6)
- *"Does this offend you?"* (Jn 6:61)
- *"If I am telling the truth, why don't you believe me?"* (Jn 8:46)
- *"Will you lay down your life for me?"* (Jn 13:38 ESV)
- *"Who are you looking for?"* (Jn 18:4, 7 NLT)

Sometimes I sit with each of these questions for a week or longer. I imagine Jesus asking me directly and personally, *What do you actually want? Who are you looking for?* It has ushered in deeply personal and conversational times of prayer.

The second way is to utilize five questions to guide my Bible reading process. Somewhere along my spiritual journey, though I don't remember where, I was introduced to five questions we can ask every time we read the Bible.

- *What is going on in this passage?*
- *What do I like about the passage, or what am I encouraged about?*
- *What disturbs me or startles me in this passage?*
- *What does this reveal about the nature of God or the character of Jesus?*
- *What will I do with what I've just read in the next seven days?*

I've used these to guide a discussion with someone who was reading the Bible for the first time as well as with students in the seminary courses I taught. It frames our time of engagement and cultivates a posture of receptive expectancy and joyful obedience.

Taking it a bit further, when I read the stories of Jesus and even the parables Jesus teaches, I like to ask a subset of questions:

- *If I closed my eyes and imagined being a participant or an observer in the story, what do I notice?*
- *What does the setting sound, smell, look, taste, and feel like?*
- *What do I sense, perceive, or feel? Am I excited? Nervous? Fearful? Joyful? Something else?*
- *What might have motivated Jesus to tell this story, and why to those people in particular?*
- *Who do I relate to the most in this story, and why that person?*

But one of my favorite and most formative practices is a Jewish practice called *chavruta.* The Hebrew word means friendship, partnership, or conversation partner. It's a participatory Scripture practice usually done in pairs in which partners discuss, analyze, explore, and even debate a passage together. Oftentimes this practice occurs in a yeshiva, a school that studies Torah, but it can also be done with friends or family members.

While this is commonplace for Jews, it can feel unnatural for Christians, who often assume that asking questions about the Bible reveals a weak faith. Additionally, in our traditional Western educational style, a teacher stands before a group of students to lecture. In *chavruta*, the learning is participatory and relies heavily on students' self-discovery, which is most often done by asking questions of the text. The practice forces us to think critically, not passively (and keeps us from falling asleep). It helps to deepen thought and broaden faith in God, even when we don't know all the answers. This practice is not intended to cultivate doubt or disbelief but instead to encourage us to dig for treasures in the text that can only be unearthed when we ask questions.

Years ago, a rabbi in Jerusalem first introduced me to this practice. One of the assignments he gave us was to read an Old Testament passage and generate a list of questions about the text. We were encouraged to discuss with our classmates, share our questions, and bring them to class the next week. It took some getting used to because it was so wildly different from other assignments we'd been given. It was hard to push away the instincts that had been drilled into our heads for years: to only provide correct answers, to not share our learnings with other classmates, to regurgitate what we learned from the teacher, etc. Up to that point, my entire educational experience had been evaluated on the quality of the answers I'd given. This was the first time I was evaluated on the quality of my questions. And yet, through *chavruta,* I saw things in the text I had never noticed before and learned new things about God's story.

I continue to engage in *chavruta* regularly—sometimes in groups, other times on my own. It continues to be enlightening and eye-opening. For example, when I was studying the story of Abraham sacrificing Isaac in Genesis 22, I spent time trying to generate a list of one hundred questions about the text. It was a significant challenge, but it was deeply rewarding. How grueling was the hike up the mountain, especially for the servants carrying the wood for the burnt offering? What was running through Abraham's head and heart on the climb up? What was the look on Isaac's face when Abraham told him that he would be the sacrifice? How big was his knife?

But then I started pressing in further. Jews call this story the *Aqedah* (Hebrew for "the binding of Isaac"), but Christians call it the sacrifice of Isaac. Should we also call it the *Aqedah*? What did the angel's voice sound like when he called out to stop Abraham? What was the interaction like between Abraham and Sarah when Abraham returned home? And why would God command Abraham to kill his own son when he would later give Israel a list of ten commandments, one of which was explicitly not to kill?

Every time I engage in *chavruta*, I'm left with more questions than answers. Some of these questions are uncomfortable, but they help me to perceive this story and many others with fresh eyes. I never would have seen this story through all these angles if I hadn't engaged in *chavruta*.

One of the most straightforward ways to learn to ask questions like Jesus did is to intentionally study the questions he asked. Read through a red-letter edition of the Gospels and circle every red question mark you find. Then step back and ask yourself:

- *What prompted Jesus to ask this question?*
- *Who did he direct his question to?*
- *What was his goal and purpose to ask rather than to tell?*
- *What impact did it have? And what impact might it have on us today?*
- *Are there patterns or themes in what he asked that are worth paying attention to?*

Once you begin to notice the questions of Jesus, you'll also notice the questions other people asked Jesus. For example, during Easter weekend this past year, I read the interaction between Jesus and Pilate in the Gospels. I noticed something I hadn't before: in the book of Matthew, Pilate asked six questions—and when he saw he was getting nowhere and that an uproar had started, he made only two brief statements. The books of Luke and John include several questions from Pilate as well as several statements. John includes the most famous of Pilate's questions: "What is truth?" (Jn 18:38). Mark records that Pilate asked seven questions and made no statements at all. The number of questions Pilate asked—of Jesus, the religious leaders, and the crowd—helped me to see him in a slightly different light than I had before as one who was exploring, listening, discerning, and questioning who Jesus truly was. This occurred because I was looking for the questions other people asked Jesus. Another idea worth exploring: study the questions the disciples asked Jesus and see what you notice.

You may want to do a deeper dive in studying some of the specific questions of Jesus. This takes some time and investment, but it can be significantly formative and eye-opening. For example, in the Gospel of John, the author uses "tags" at the end of questions by inserting the Greek word *me* to anticipate a potentially negative answer or one that implies doubt. It challenges the recipient to be curious and wrestle with what they are reading. Some of the recorded questions end with *can he? do you? does he? have they? is he?* or *are you?* Such as, "Surely he can't be the Messiah, can he?" (Jn 4:29 NET) and "The Christ doesn't come from Galilee, does he?" (Jn 7:41, NET). The fourth Gospel was written so that people would believe Jesus is the Christ (Jn 20:31), so it should come as no surprise that John's questions are worded with a posture of seeking, wondering, and wrestling with who Jesus is.

Several years ago, I attended a pastors' conference in San Diego. One afternoon I went to a breakout session attended by a few dozen other pastors, where the presenter asked a question that broke me open.

"Close your eyes," she instructed us, "and imagine that God is thinking specifically about you." After a moment of silence, she asked slowly, "What is the expression on God's face as he thinks about you?"

The question pierced me like few questions before. I'd always believed God loves me. I'd taught and preached about God's love for years, but without fully naming it, I'd also believed that God loves me only because he has to. He loves me, but he doesn't *like* me. I lived believing that God was either tolerating having me around or was deeply disappointed with me—slightly annoyed and all too aware of my myriad shortcomings, sin, and lack of growth.

But in that moment, I caught a clear glimpse of God's face beaming with joy and pride, a look glowing with compassion and love—*for me*. Here I was, a pastor, a professional Christian paid to love Jesus and tell others about his love for them, and yet for the first time, I was able to see that God actually *liked* me. I was able to receive the love he had been wanting to extend to me for years. I couldn't hold back. I wept loudly from the back row, something releasing in me that had been pent up for years. It wasn't yet another sermon on grace or forgiveness or redemption that changed me; it was a reflective question. This question remains so powerful and significant that I return to it frequently to be reminded of my belovedness.

We don't stunt our spiritual formation by asking questions. We stunt our formation when we don't.

PART 4

RIDICULOUSLY PRACTICAL WAYS TO ASK BETTER QUESTIONS

What is the best question you've been asked this month?

What is the best question you've asked someone else this month?

Who do you know who asks great questions?

When was the last time someone said to you, "You know, you ask really great questions"?

What would it take for you to be someone who asks great questions?

How do we ask questions that are both timeless and timely?

Which is more important in the question-asking process: What we ask, who we ask, when we ask, or how we ask?

How might the discipline of asking better questions expand and enrich the human experience?

10

PREPARING TO ASK BETTER QUESTIONS

How can we grow to ask better questions?

No man really becomes a fool until he stops asking questions.

CHARLES PROTEUS STEINMETZ

*Our lives are living out answers to questions
we don't notice that we were asking. Asking different
questions helps us lead different lives.*

JENNIFER GARVEY BERGER

HOW DO WE DEVELOP THE SKILLS to ask better questions? In this final portion of the book, I include a wide variety of ridiculously practical ways you can grow to ask better questions. These three chapters are divided into practices you can engage in before asking questions of others: *preparation* (chapter 10)—practices you can utilize while you are asking other people questions; *participation* (chapter 11); and then *reflection* (chapter 12)—reflective exercises to help you consider the quality of the questions you've asked.

But before we get there, I need to say this: *If you want to ask better questions, you have to begin with genuine interest in others.* Curiosity is fundamentally at the center of questions. If we don't possess genuine curiosity, these practices won't matter all that much in the long run.

But even a genuine interest in others is still not enough. We need specific and intentional practices rooted in our everyday lives. Call them what you want—practices, habits, exercises, spiritual disciplines, action steps—but we grow when we live out specific actions in an embodied form, because training takes us further than just trying.

My purpose is to encourage form without a formula and intention without an equation. I don't know which practices will work best for you. If some of the practices don't resonate, then just keep reading. But if you land on one that's helpful, circle it and make a note. Experiment with it. Try it on for size. Invite others to participate in it with you. You can try some of these individually or communally. Read these next few chapters like you eat seafood: swallow the meat and spit out the bones. You get to decide what is meat and what are the bones. Just don't choke on the bones. And don't try to do all of these all at once—you'll get overwhelmed and set yourself up for failure.

Here are nine practices you can engage in to help prepare you to ask great questions.

1. KEEP A QUESTIONS JOURNAL

One of people's biggest misconceptions is that they have to generate all the questions themselves. Good news: you don't. Your job is to collect the best questions available from anywhere you can find them. Some of the best questions I've come across I've gleaned from podcast interviews, a friend's social media post, a book, a waitress at a restaurant, a television commercial, a panel discussion at a conference I attended, listening to children at the playground, reading an interstate billboard, and overhearing two women chatting behind me in line at a coffee shop.

When you stumble on a thoughtful question, the simplest and most important thing you can do is to write it down immediately. (No, you won't remember it later.) In a journal, on an index card, or in the notes section of your phone—it doesn't matter. Just find something you can access and record quickly and easily. I was watching an episode of Jerry

Seinfeld's television series *Comedians in Cars Getting Coffee* where he interviewed Dana Carvey. As they sat in a restaurant booth drinking coffee and laughing, Carvey paused and asked Seinfeld, "When do you feel most fully loved?" Immediately, I pressed pause and grabbed my notebook.

The last two pages of my notebook have always been reserved for questions I'm currently asking myself or I've recently gleaned from others. In my current journal I have forty-seven so far. Here are a few:

- *Am I being productive, or am I just being busy?*
- *Is it well with my soul?*
- *When am I at my best?*
- *What is my favorite mistake, and what did I learn from it?*
- *What questions am I trying to answer in this season?*
- *Who do I long to become? What gets in the way of that process of becoming?*
- *What am I measuring to tell me if my day was successful or not?*
- *What do I know now that I wish I knew when I graduated from college?*
- *What is it like to sit across the table from me?*
- *When and where do I feel angry? Inadequate? Fearful? Hopeful?*

If any of the questions above are helpful, write them down. As your list grows, review your questions regularly, asking yourself:

- *Why did these questions intrigue me enough to write them down?*
- *Are there any patterns I'm noticing in the questions here?*
- *What should I do with these questions and my answers?*
- *Which questions could I ask of whom in the next week?*

Give yourself a challenge: try and collect three significant questions in a given week. Once your radar is up, you'll be attuned to listen for them.

2. BE PURPOSEFULLY AWARE OF THE FOUR LEVELS OF QUESTIONS AND LOOK FOR WAYS TO LEVEL UP

In chapter three we explored the four levels of questions. If you can think about the framework of the four levels, both with the questions you ask and those you hear others asking, your awareness will continue to increase. (Feel free to go back and review those levels.) As you hear coworkers talking in the breakroom, or as you listen to a host interviewing a guest on a podcast, or as you sit around the family dinner table, pause and ask yourself, *What level was that question?*

More importantly, consider your own questions. *What questions did I ask, and which levels were they on?* Think about how you could be just a bit more thoughtful, focused, and specific with your questions. Challenge yourself to take things to the next level. Table 10.1 includes some examples.

Table 10.1. Asking next-level questions

Common question	Next-level question
How are you?	What's been the most interesting part of your day thus far?
Where did you grow up?	What was the best part of where you grew up?
Where did you attend college?	What were your most formative experiences in college?
How was your vacation?	What was the most exciting experience or meaningful memory from your recent vacation?
Where do you work?	What are you currently working on that you're finding interesting or deeply satisfying?
Where do you live?	How might you describe your neighborhood in three adjectives?
What do you do for a living?	How did you end up doing what you do for a living?
How was your Father's Day?	What's the most meaningful part of being a father?
What do you like to do for fun?	If you had an entire Saturday with no responsibilities whatsoever on the calendar, what would you want to do?

Perhaps in a presentation at work last week, you finished by asking the team, "Any thoughts?" (a Level One question) and, not surprisingly, you were rewarded with blank stares and awkward silence. In your next presentation, try leveling up and ending your presentation by asking more focused and intentional questions such as, "Based on what we've covered today, what questions remain that I can help answer?" or "What was most clear for you in this presentation, and where might there still be confusion that I can help clarify before we end?" Or better still: "Based on what we discussed together here, what implications does this have for the current project we're working on?"

With just 5 or 10 percent more intention and effort, you can level up and make a noticeable improvement in your questions. Ask more interesting questions, and you'll get more interesting answers. Ask and you shall receive.

As you level up your questions, keep in mind that doing so will require a bit more investment and time. More thoughtful questions are not five-second responses that we give as we pass a coworker in the hallway. We may need the time and space to unpack these thoughtful questions over coffee, lunch, or on a long walk. The deeper the possibility for genuine connection, the more likely it is that it will take some time.

3. THINK PURPOSEFULLY ABOUT COMMON QUESTIONS TO AVOID

We're all prone to ask lazy questions. "How ya doing?," "What's up?," and "How are you?" are the most frequent offenders. *What are the questions you ask out of habit but aren't all that helpful, thoughtful, or meaningful?* Write them down and make a commitment to remove them from your vocabulary as much as possible. Consider generating a better question you could replace it with. Sure, we use "How are you doing?" as a culturally implied acknowledgment of someone's presence, but the question is limp and thoughtless. Because of this, I've replaced it with a simple "Good to see you" or "Hello there" instead. Or, if I do ask, "How are you doing?" I try to make sure I ask it authentically, truly desiring to hear a response.

While I made a commitment long ago to avoid a few of my own lazy questions, on occasion I slip back into bad habits. My son and I were running errands recently, and as we were checking out, I thoughtlessly asked the cashier, "How ya doing?" Without looking up, she offered a rote and uninspiring response: "Fine." Realizing I had just asked a lazy question that was on my no-fly-zone list, I quickly considered how I could salvage the interaction. I smiled and asked, "Do you mean it?" She looked up at me with a surprised smile, thought for a moment, and said, "Yeah, I think I'm doing all right," as she placed our items in a bag. "I get off my shift in about thirty minutes. Then I'm going home to relax." She told me she was looking forward to curling up on the couch with her dog and watching a movie to unwind after a long day. She shared a bit more of herself, and we laughed together before we left. It wasn't long, no more than a minute, but it made for a more meaningful interaction for all three of us. It's amazing how the conversation goes to another level if we're just a bit more intentional and thoughtful about our questions.

4. PREPARE A FEW QUESTIONS
BEFORE YOUR NEXT MEETING

Think about your next meeting, whether it's for work or connecting with a friend, and the person or people who will be there. What are they going through? What do they know that you don't? What are you assuming will be accomplished in your time together? Then jot down a couple of questions you could potentially ask in your meeting. Charles Duhigg suggests asking yourself a few specific questions of yourself before the conversation begins: *How do I hope things will unfold? What obstacles might emerge? What are the benefits of this discussion?* You don't have to ask every question you're prepared to ask—and many times, you might not ask them at all. That's okay. You'll still work your questions muscle and be even more prepared next time you meet with someone. I don't suggest you bring notecards full of questions to your meeting, but if you do, make it subtle and natural.

When I've shared this practice with others, some people have pushed back because it seems to be a bit extreme, a little too much effort. Of course, we want to avoid making any interaction feel forced or manufactured, and we all have limited time and energy. But I have found that when I can bring just a bit more intention and thought to my conversations, they are almost always interesting, fruitful, and more meaningful than if I hadn't come prepared.

When you're interviewing for a job, always come prepared with at least a few questions to ask your potential employer. Job interviews should be a two-way street. When I interview people for an open position, I always end by asking, "Do you have any questions you'd like to ask us?" If they say no, I am significantly less likely to hire them. It shows me something that gives me pause. I want people on my team who are genuinely curious and prepared to engage.

5. IDENTIFY QUESTION MENTORS
YOU CAN LEARN FROM

Who do you know who asks great questions? What makes them skilled question-askers? What are the types of questions they ask? If you're fortunate to know the individuals who came to mind, treat them to lunch or coffee and ask them how they became great question-askers. Inquire about what they do to purposefully sharpen their question-asking skills. Find out why they're motivated to ask good questions, where they learned the skill, and how they grow in the craft. (And, of course, go into these conversations with a few questions that you've prepared ahead of time.) If you named good question-askers who you don't know personally, there are still ways you could learn from them. Are they an author or speaker? Learn from the resources they've published or produced, send them an email, or reach out on social media.

When I was in high school, I studied Larry King, the legendary interviewer and host of *Larry King Live*, which aired nightly on CNN for twenty seasons for over sixty-one hundred episodes. He interviewed over fifty thousand celebrities, politicians, leaders, and other fascinating people throughout his career. Many times on his show, the people he interviewed would share personally and vulnerably while millions watched at home. I love watching his show, and I've reread his book on several occasions. In addition to paying close attention to his questions, I even studied his body language during interviews. This might seem excessive, but I learned a lot about asking questions from one of the best, even though I never met him.

6. DEVELOP FIVE TO TEN HIGH-QUALITY QUESTIONS YOU CAN ACCESS EASILY

Maybe you desire to grow in your question-asking ability, but you aren't quick on your feet. You struggle to think of a good question in the moment and then kick yourself when you think of a good one five minutes after the conversation is over. Your frustration is understandable, and you're not alone. This is why I strongly encourage you to develop an easily accessible list.

You can have it handy in your wallet, your purse, on an index card, or in a note in your phone—or you can try and memorize several of them. Having a mental list in your literal or metaphorical pocket can be valuable. High-quality questions are not generic, yet they can be utilized in almost any situation or conversation.

A few high-quality questions I've used in my interactions with others have included:

- *What's the best book you've read in the past six months?*
- *On a scale of one to ten—one being low and ten being high—how does your job rate on your passion meter? What would make that number higher if something were to change?*
- *In three adjectives, how would you describe your day/week/month?*
- *What are the things you're excited or intrigued about currently?*
- *What are you looking forward to these days?*

- *What are the hopes and aspirations you have about your family/ future/company/career?*

Think of what you would want to draw out of others, what you would want to know about them, and what would lead them to feel valued as individuals. However, if you're still struggling to remember anything on your list and you're in a conversation drawing a blank, here are two that you can use with confidence: "I want to get to know you better. What question do you hope people ask you about your life?" and "What's your story?" Creating safe spaces for people to honestly and courageously share what's on their mind or tell their story is one of the best gifts you can give to others. And don't be surprised if people thank you for going beyond the predictable surface-level questions they're used to hearing.

7. LATCH ONTO A GRAND QUESTION AND WRESTLE WITH IT FOR SIX MONTHS OR LONGER

We often learn more by looking for the answer to a question and not finding it than we do from learning the answer itself. This is the beauty of beholding a Grand Question. It is a question that must be discerned over a long period of time or can't be answered easily, yet it is worth wrestling with nonetheless.

Sometimes I've latched onto a Grand Question and wrestled with it for six months or more. Some of them have included *Where does leadership end and manipulation begin? What does meekness look like in our culture, and who do I know who is meek? Why is it that the more right I think I am, the less kind I think I have to be?* I journal about it. Sometimes I write it on an index card and carry it around with me. I ponder it when I am on a walk, sitting in traffic, or folding laundry. I ask other thoughtful, wise people what they think about it and if they have any insights to share.

Sometimes I'm able to come to a clear and compelling answer, but it's been stress tested and refined over a long period. At other times, the questions simply cannot be answered sufficiently, no matter how long I reflect on them—and that's okay. Poet David Whyte describes them as "questions that have patiently waited for you, questions that have no right to go away." Asking a Grand Question often opens up stimulating conversations with others. See if you can find a few conversation partners who would enjoy these fruitful discussions and ask them what Grand Questions they're wrestling with as well.

8. WRITE QUESTIONS IN THE MARGINS OF YOUR BOOKS (INCLUDING THIS ONE)

When I read a book, I always have a pen in hand. I butcher my books with earmarks, dog-ears, underlines, circles, stars, and scribbled notes in the margins. I write down a lot of questions too. I'm certainly not the first to do this. It was purported that John Adams wrote in the margins of his books—so many words that at times his own words outnumbered the printed words on the page.

Consider yourself a conversation partner with the author of any book. This mindset helps you to better process what you're learning. I sometimes try to imagine myself sharing a meal with them (even if they have passed away) and enjoying the opportunity to ask about what they've written. I wonder where the author first developed that particular assumption. Or how this thought might affect how I think about my relationship with my sons. Or if I could try this idea out in my organization. Whether or not you're able to ask the author questions personally is beside the point. What would you *want* to ask them if you could?

Sometimes you actually can. I've emailed my questions to several authors after reading their books, and many have been kind enough to write me back. You can email me if you'd like. My contact information is in the back of the book. Sometimes my questions scribbled in the margins are directed toward the author. Other times, I write down what I want to challenge myself with when I finish the book. Still other times the questions are rhetorical or theoretical. Or I stumble upon a new Grand Question to carry with me.

9. ENGAGE IN A QUESTIONS AUDIT

Finally, engage in a questions audit. Like athletes who go back and watch their game tapes, you can engage in an audit to help you grow in your ability and awareness. Recount the questions you ask of yourself, God, and others as best you can. Let's say you notice you're asking the same worn-out questions over and over, or you ask ones you don't really care to know the answer to. For the next week, do a questions audit. *What exactly did I ask? Were my questions more informative or incisive in nature? Did they add value, deepen connection, or help me to discover or learn something new?* You may consider broadening it beyond just a questions audit to a conversation audit. Think about the shift-response and support-response concepts in chapter three. Identifying the questions you asked and the type of responses you offered will help you to become aware of your question-asking and conversational tendencies.

Now, let me encourage you to go back through the chapter and review the nine practices.

Which one or two practices could you experiment with in the next few weeks?

ENGAGING WITH QUESTIONS

What can we be aware of in our conversations with others?

What if instead of seeing questions as the keys that unlock answers,
we saw answers as stepping stones to the next questions?

Ed Catmull

We thought that we had the answers,
it was the questions we had wrong.

"11 O'clock Tick Tock" by U2

I N THE LAST CHAPTER we explored the practices you can engage in *prior* to asking questions of others. But there are things you can do *while* you're asking questions in real time. It takes some additional effort, but it's important to be fully present with others while also thinking of ways to enhance your question-asking.

Here are twenty specific practices to help you increase your capacity for inquiry. The first section outlines steps you can take to ask yourself, and the second section includes practices you can do with others.

ASKING QUESTIONS OF YOURSELF

1. Identify your motives. We must ask ourselves the questions *behind* the questions. *Have I established trust with this person to ask these questions? Is this the right time to ask? Does this person even want to be asked questions?* The right question asked at the wrong time can become the wrong question.

Because questions are so forceful, it's also important to be keenly aware of our motivations. *Why am I about to ask this? To what end?* There are many reasons why we could ask a question: to learn new information, to make someone feel comfortable, or to genuinely connect with someone. Or it could be to subtly express our opinion, to try to impress others, to put someone on the defensive, or to trap them with their own words. It's important to step back and consider, *Am I trying to sound smart? Am I trying to trick someone? Or am I genuinely interested?* It's amazing what you can learn if you listen to your response. It may also keep you from saying something you'll regret later.

2. Think carefully about the wording and tone of your questions. Oftentimes, we focus so much on what we say that we forget the significance and weight of how we say it. This includes our volume, tone, eye contact, and body language. When we change the emphasis placed on the words of a question, we can change its meaning and elicit different emotions. Consider this:

- *How* could you say that? (Inquiring about the style or manner in which something could be communicated)
- How *could* you say that? (A reprimand, as in "How dare you say that!")
- How could *you* say that? ("Others can say what you just said, but not you.")
- How could you *say* that? ("You may be able to think it, but voicing it is rude.")
- How could you say *that*? (Questioning the credibility or accuracy of what was just said)

The same five words with an emphasis on a different word create five different meanings. Think carefully about both the *what* and the *how*. The right question asked the wrong way can become the wrong question.

3. Think about head, heart, and hands. It's best to think about the three categories of questions we could ask others: head, heart, and hands. Questions about the head center around thoughts or information. These could include stats or straightforward data. Heart questions focus on feelings and emotions and often include stories or experiences. Hands questions are often action oriented, implying *What's next?* or *What will we do now?* The best question-askers seek to intersperse questions from all three categories. Varying these appropriately in conversation helps to engage the whole person.

4. Track your Q/A ratio. One of the best ways to assess how well you listen in conversation is to track your Question/Answer ratio. Years ago, when I participated in training to become a leadership coach, I was required to track my Q/A ratio for each coaching conversation I participated in. We were taught that in a coaching conversation, we should adhere to the 15:85 principle. Coaches should be asking questions and briefly offering a few thoughts, insights, and resources for about 15 percent of the conversation, while the remaining 85 percent of the time the person being coached should be doing the talking.

Of course, most interactions are not coaching conversations, so this ratio does not always apply. A better ratio to aim for in everyday conversations might be 40:60, where you take on the responsibility to be the better question-asker in the conversation. Regardless, the point is to be aware of your Q/A ratio. Tracking it gives you a strong indication of how you are doing in conversations with others. Two good questions to ask after a meeting or a one-on-one conversation are *Did I talk most of the time, or did I listen?* and *What percentage of my time did I ask questions or share?* Simply being aware of your ratio can help to sharpen your awareness and your ability to ask questions at the right time in the right amount. As mentioned in chapter eight, think like a midwife.

5. *Genuinely ask because you care—or don't ask at all.* Sometimes we ask questions we really don't care to hear the answer to; we're just being polite. At times we feel compelled to ask a question for the sake of social graces. We *should* be kind to others, most assuredly. But sometimes we have to ask ourselves, *Are we wasting our time here? Am I being disingenuous or untruthful in this situation?* We don't often give others enough credit; most people can tell when they're being asked a question by someone who doesn't really care to know the answer. Testing our motives before we ask questions can be a refining process and can keep us from asking questions we should not ask. A good principle to live by: if you aren't genuinely interested or don't care about someone's answer, then it's probably best to not ask it.

Conversely, you may have been in conversations where someone asked you a thoughtful question and you felt honored by the gesture. You opened your mouth to share, only to be interrupted by the person who asked, who then shared their answer to their own question. It's demeaning, isn't it? You realize they were simply looking for a platform to express their own ideas and opinions. This bad habit is called *boomerasking*, another form of conversational narcissism where you throw out a question fully expecting it to come right back to you. I know people who ask well-worded and thoughtful questions. The problem is they're simply asking themselves questions to set up answers they want to share with others. (The exception to this principle, of course, is an appropriately utilized rhetorical question.) When we ask others a thoughtful question, we need to shut up and let them answer.

6. *Ask yourself significant questions during times of failure.* Failure can really take a bite out of our heart and soul, but it also provides fertile ground for growth. During failure it's easy to jump to conclusions, blame and shame, or be tempted to believe lies about ourselves or others. One way to steward failure well is to take the time to process that failure honestly and courageously with questions.

Helpful questions to consider when processing failure could be:

- *Why did this project/initiative/decision/action fail? What factors contributed to this outcome?*

- *What implications does this have on me (emotionally, mentally, spiritually, physically, relationally, vocationally, etc.) and on others?*

- *What parts of the failure do I need to own? What parts of the failure do I need to let go of?*

- *What can I learn from this? If I were to do it again, how would I do it differently?*

- *What other trusted individuals can I process this with in a healthy and beneficial manner?*

7. Engage with the Jewish Scripture practice of chavruta. In chapter nine, we explored the Jewish Scripture-reading practice of *chavruta*, which involves reading a passage and then listing out as many questions as possible. If you want to try it yourself, consider starting with a few Old Testament stories, such as Noah and the flood, Jacob wrestling with God, or Joseph being reunited with his brothers in Egypt. Remember: don't offer any answers. Just ask questions. To get started, you could use these prompts: *I wonder why . . . I'm curious about . . . Why was this detail included in the story? Why isn't anything said about . . . ?* This practice can be done by yourself or with friends, colleagues, or family members.

8. Gamify your growth. Whether catching up with a friend over coffee, sitting through a meeting, or working with a leader in a coaching session, I play a game with myself. I try to ask thoughtful, meaningful, and sometimes provocative questions that will elicit a response such as:

- *That's a good question* [often followed by thoughtful silence].

- *Hmm, I've never been asked that before.*

- *Wow. Let me think about that and get back to you.*

- *You ask really good questions.*

- *Thank you for asking.*

If someone responds in one of these ways, I give myself a point. Sure, it may sound a bit silly, but it's one of the simplest and best ways I push myself to improve as a question-asker. I assure you: I'm genuinely listening in conversations. I want others to feel honored, to go to a place within themselves they haven't gone before or to see a possibility they hadn't previously considered. But here's the thing: *you can't tell anybody else you're playing this game.* If you do, it ruins the game completely. It's simply a way you can challenge yourself to grow. And if you receive any of these responses, silently give yourself a point and take it as affirmation you're asking important and meaningful questions. When you ask a thoughtful question everyone wins, including you.

ASKING QUESTIONS OF OTHERS

1. Ask people about their hopes, dreams, and passions. One of the most important ways to value others is to ask questions directed toward the heart. When we create a safe place for people to share about their passions, aspirations, dreams, fears, and hopes, they get excited. When I do this, people's answers are most often intriguing, personal, and inspiring.

I once asked a woman about her hopes and dreams for her and her family's future. After several minutes of passionate and excited sharing, she paused midsentence, looked at me, and said, "Thank you for asking. Nobody has ever asked me this before." Then she quickly returned to telling me more. Having people open up to share their hopes and dreams is a gift. But inquirer, beware: since it's so rare for people to be asked a thoughtful, heartfelt question, be prepared to listen for a long time. People have a lot to share but few safe places to share it.

2. Avoid asking closed-ended questions. Sometimes I think, *How can I ask this question in a way that would make it difficult to elicit a simple one-word answer?* This is especially true when I ask my teenage sons about their day. Asking, "So, how was your day at school?" elicits predictable one-word, or closed, responses: "Fine." "Good." "Okay." Or just a shrug, sigh, or grunt.

Instead, I try to ask them questions that would be almost impossible to answer with just one word. *What is one interesting thing that happened at school? What's something you learned today that you didn't know when you woke up this morning? In three adjectives, how would you describe school today?* These types of questions are focused yet open-ended enough that they can take it any direction they'd like; I am just there to listen without an agenda. Open-ended, or divergent, questions are versatile and robust. Former FBI hostage negotiator Chris Voss said that an open-ended question is one of the bureau's most potent negotiating tools. It works in everyday situations too.

Many people feel we shouldn't start questions with "why" because it could potentially sound off-putting or put others on the defensive. I understand the sentiment, but I do believe that at appropriate times asking why can be an extremely effective way to connect. To be certain, we must make sure trust is present and ensure our tone, volume, and body language communicate genuine interest and curiosity. When I coach leaders who want to grow in their ability to ask good questions, I encourage them to think like a three-year-old by asking why more often than anyone else (while also making sure they don't annoy or frustrate others the way three-year-olds do with that question). Ask why more often . . . but not too much.

3. Hit the ball back over the net. A good conversation is like tennis. You share, then hit the ball to the other person. They, in turn, share and hit it back to you. Back and forth it goes. When someone asks you a question, and after you've answered it, one of the easiest things you can do is to just hit the ball back over the net. You do this by asking, "What about you?" or "How would you answer that question?" It's amazing how many times someone answers a good question but doesn't turn it back around to the original asker. Oftentimes, people who are asking a thoughtful question are also wishing to be asked it as well.

A few times a year, after finishing a meal with someone, an unsettling thought hits me: *I wasn't asked a single question the entire time.* I feel a pinch of confusion, sadness, and loneliness. Over the course of our time together, there were numerous opportunities when, after I asked a question or two, a noticeable lull occurred, an opening in the conversation to ask something. But a question never came. I asked them questions to learn more about them, but the truth is I wanted that person to ask me about my perspective as well. All they had to do was ask that simple question before they took another bite of their buffalo chicken wrap: *What about you?* It takes just three words to hit the ball back over the net.

4. Ask follow-up questions. Oftentimes, the magic isn't found in the first question but in the second or third. When someone responds to your initial question, follow up with another:

- *Really?*
- *Wow, that's interesting. What was that like?*
- *Why's that?*
- *Have you always felt this way?*
- *How did that make you feel?*
- *Is there anything else you want to share?*
- *And then what happened?*

This type of short question is sometimes called a sluice. A sluice is a small water channel containing a movable gate in which the water flow and level can be managed. When we ask keen follow-up questions we are, in a sense, managing the flow and level of the conversation.

5. Instill in your children the passion and skill of asking questions. One of the best gifts parents can give their children is a passion for asking and engaging in great questions. It's been said that more is caught than taught. Growing up, I observed and learned many valuable lessons from my parents. One of those was the magic that happens when someone, especially my father, asks a good question. I watched him ask genuine, thoughtful, intentional questions of others at church, in our neighborhood, and around the dinner table—and I saw how others received those questions as a gift. On the rare occasion I encounter a kid who asks good questions, especially around adults, I usually learn later that their parents were intentional in cultivating a question-asking ethos at home.

There are several rhythms and practices we've cultivated in our two sons' lives with questions in three areas: mealtime, drive time, and bedtime.

Mealtime: Over the years, our family has purchased several books that are filled with questions and conversation starters. Occasionally, we'll pull one out and ask two or three age-appropriate questions while we eat. It makes for great dinner conversations, teaches us all about the importance of listening, and creates space for us to learn new things about each other. Sometimes we ask the highs and lows of the day. I know of some families that regularly engage in "rose, thorn, bud" (one good thing from your day, one bad thing from your day, and one thing you're looking forward to tomorrow).

Drive time: Car rides have been one of the best ways to connect with my sons. It's been said that females engage most naturally in conversation face to face, while males engage most naturally shoulder to shoulder—and I think there's some truth to that. Looking out the front windshield has allowed for purposeful on-the-way conversation. Turn off the podcast, encourage everyone to put away the earbuds, ask an intentional question, and see what happens.

Bedtime: When our sons were little, I added something called "question of the night" to their bedtime routine. For a time, our boys shared a room with a bunk bed. At bedtime, my wife and I read books to each of them, prayed, and then hugged and kissed them good night. But I added a new twist: I would turn out the lights, lie on my back next to them, and for the next few minutes ask them a question. I would ask about their favorite sport, if they'd ever felt scared at school, or what they wanted to be when they grow up. Then they had the opportunity to ask me any question they wanted. They would ask what my favorite color was, what position I played in little league, and if I have any regrets in life. Sometimes the conversations were brief and silly, other times deeply significant, carrying over into multiple nights.

Whatever rhythms work with your family, try to intentionally cultivate spaces where both parents and children can ask questions.

6. Hold a questions-only conversation with others. When I lead training events around question-asking, we often engage in a playful exercise in which the only rule is that every sentence in the conversation must end with a question mark. There's always a slightly awkward sense at the start, a feeling of collective silliness, but we eventually settle in. It forces us to think carefully about how quickly we want to rush to make statements and nudges us to be more thoughtful with our questions.

Theater companies and comedy improv utilize this strategy for training and during live performances. Why? It keeps the dialogue going, and the open-ended nature allows performances to go in a variety of possible directions. It's often quite hilarious. Set a timer for five minutes. Don't worry about the awkwardness—just try it. You'll grow in your questions and enjoy a good laugh or two in the process.

7. Ask people about their tattoos. One of the most practical, easy, and creepy-free ways to connect with people you don't know is to ask about their ink. Any time someone has spent good money and voluntarily experienced physical pain to have something affixed permanently to their body, it means it's important to them.

People love to tell you about their ink. In fact, I've never had a single person turn me down. If they have several tattoos, I like to ask which one is the most meaningful to them. A waitress in Canada showed me her arm and told me about her undying love for her six cats; a bartender in Chicago rolled up his sleeve and shared how he used to be a pastor but left his faith entirely after he experienced abuse; and a cashier at a thrift store in my community gently tapped the inside of her wrist as she tearfully shared how much she missed her father, who had passed away several years ago. The conversations are rich, naturally opening up a path for others to share what holds deep meaning in their lives.

8. *Play question roulette*. Start by writing down a list of thoughtful questions in a journal or in the notes section of your phone. Let's say you've created a total of twenty-seven questions. When you're with your friends for dinner, tell them you'd like to ask them a question, but first you'll need them to pick any number from one to twenty-seven. If they pick number fourteen, read out the fourteenth question on your list. It's simple, but it works—and it's fun. It includes just enough structure and intentionality but with a healthy dollop of spontaneity.

9. *Engage in question-storming*. When working with a group, especially when you're facing a problem or feeling stuck on an issue, press pause. Instead of trying to find a solution, attempt to come through the backdoor. Invite people to ask only questions about the issue or problem. One group of experts calls this process "question-storming." They suggest groups should attempt to generate fifty questions about the problem at hand, and no one can ask the next question until the last one has been written down completely. After engaging in this, it's often surprising how the group can see the problem with greater clarity and thus know how to address it.

10. *Ask people of different generations what questions they ask frequently*. In chapter four, we looked at Gordon MacDonald's set of questions that people ask in different decades of their lives. (Again, the full list is in Resource 2.) But there are also different overarching questions that people of different generations ask, which are often shaped by environment, history, and culture. For example, the oldest generation today lived through World War II. A dominating question in their minds has been, "How can I serve my country to fight against foreign enemies?" But this hardly reaches the top ten questions for someone in, say, Gen Z. Instead, in a country of increasing violence within our own borders, one of their dominating questions is "Am I safe?"

I enjoy asking questions of my grandfather, who is in his nineties, as well as middle school and high school students in our church who I hang out with on Monday nights. But the questions I ask are very different, and I must shift to meet them where their overarching generational thinking resides. If you can engage with people in different generations, both old and young, ask them if they can identify their most frequent or most significant questions that shape who they are and what matters most to them. It's amazing what you can learn.

11. Spend purposeful time with children. If children are some of the best question-askers on the planet, can we humble ourselves and allow them to be our teachers? They could be kids in our church or neighborhood, our nieces and nephews, our grandchildren, or our own kids. Watch how they interact. Make note of the questions they ask and how (and to whom) they ask them. It might be tempting to write their questions off as trivial and elementary—"Why do potato chip bags make such loud crinkling noises?" "Why do people look funny when we look at them upside down?" "What might Jesus' voice have sounded like?"—but we would be wise not to. Truly ponder their questions. Consider writing down one or two of the best ones they asked in the time you spent with them. It's amazing what we can learn from the world's leading experts on questions if we let ourselves be taught.

12. Shake up the Q&A session. When I lead retreats or conference breakout sessions, there is an expectation that there will be a time of Q&A at the end. These are often fruitful. I enjoy thoughtful interaction when someone asks me a question after I've just presented.

But when I present, sometimes I like to shake things up a bit so that we conduct Q&Q sessions in which only questions and further questions can be asked. On other occasions, I'll host a Q&A session in which the *A* stands for "actions." And still other times I've held an A&Q session— answers, followed by questions around that proposed answer. If you're hosting a group, team meeting, breakout session, or event, try one of these and see what kind of learning occurs. It's fun to spice things up a bit.

If you still aren't sure what to ask, a simple approach can help. Imagine you're with a close friend. Then ask yourself, *What question would I ask them?*

Stay curious. Keep asking.

REFLECTING ON THE QUESTIONS WE'VE ASKED

How can we accurately assess the quality and value of the questions we've asked?

A wise man can learn more from a foolish question
than a fool can learn from a wise answer.

BRUCE LEE

There is nothing more dangerous than the
right answer to the wrong question.

PETER DRUCKER

A FTER A MISSION IS COMPLETED, the military partici-pates in an exercise called the after-action review. It's an oppor-tunity to review the mission by asking essential questions such as, *What was supposed to happen, and what actually happened? What worked and what didn't? What can we learn from this experience that would help us act differently next time?* We've discussed ways we can prepare to ask better questions and how we can participate in them in real time. But we also need to look back and reflect on how we did. We need to conduct our own after-action reviews.

NAME THE QUESTIONS YOU ASKED
THROUGHOUT THE DAY

Similar to how you conduct a question audit, take a few moments at the end of the day to think back or look over your schedule. *Who did you interact with? What did you talk about in your conversations? What topics or issues did you address in meetings at work?*

Then try to recollect what questions were asked and, specifically, what questions you asked others.

- *Were those questions helpful and thoughtful?*
- *Did they add value, enable connection, and express care to others?*
- *Could they have been tighter or clearer?*
- *What are some questions you could have asked but didn't? What level of questions were they?*

There may be times you can't recall if you asked any questions throughout the course of a day, and that's okay. But keep asking. Continue to push yourself to be aware of your questions. Awareness is an essential part of asking better questions.

ASK FOR SPECIFIC FEEDBACK FROM OTHERS

Feedback is the breakfast of champions. It's hard to change our behavior without frequent feedback loops. It's not just a good idea to seek out honest responses and perspectives from those we trust; it's essential for our personal growth. Ask people you spend time with frequently and those who know you well—those who are willing and able to offer their perspective, even if it stings—to provide feedback about how they experience you and your questions. And don't assume they'll tell you on their own initiative. Most people won't. Instead, be proactive and make the first move.

You can simply say to them, "I'm trying to grow to become a better question-asker. I realize I need feedback, and I wondered if you could help me." (Again, avoid the generic and unhelpful "So, what'd ya think?" question at all costs.) You might consider asking them for general feedback:

- *Overall, how would you assess my ability to ask good questions? What do you notice—good or bad, big or small?*

- *How would you assess the frequency of my questions? Am I asking too many, not enough, or just the right amount?*

- *If I were to grow in asking better questions by just 5 or 10 percent, what do you think I would need to do? What do you believe I need to stop doing?*

Or you could ask them for specific feedback:

- *In yesterday's department meeting, I asked a few questions of the team to clarify the issue we are trying to solve. Did you feel like those were the right questions to be asked at the right time? Would there have been a better time to ask them?*

- *When we had lunch together with the group last week, did you feel I was talking too much, or did you feel I was asking and listening well?*

- *What question was particularly helpful? What wasn't?*

- *In the future, what is one specific, practical thing I can do at work that you believe would enhance my question-asking and benefit our team?*

This last question is not feedback but feedforward. Feedback is helpful, but feedforward can be even more formative. People are sometimes reluctant to offer feedback, as it may sound critical or judgmental, but people are often more willing to offer their thoughts concerning the future because it feels safer and more theoretical.

ASK GOD TO HELP YOU GROW IN BECOMING A BETTER QUESTION-ASKER

You may never have thought of yourself as a question-asker or aspired to become better at asking questions until reading this book. But let me encourage you to think of yourself that way moving forward, because being a better question-asker is a gift to everyone you interact with and will make you a better person in every sphere of life. And as you desire to grow in your questions, it's best to go to the source to ask for help.

When I lead trainings, I share many of the principles and practices you've read in the past three chapters. Near the end of our time together I ask, "Show of hands: how many of you regularly ask God to give you the passion and the skill to ask better questions?" In all the years I've asked this, never once has someone raised their hand.

For the past several years, I've made it a regular practice to ask God for help, guidance, and wisdom to ask better questions. I ask that he would make me the best question-asker in North America. On the surface, this might sound odd and slightly self-centered. Of course, there's no national question-asking contest where ribbons are handed out. I don't pray this for my own glory or recognition. Instead, I ask boldly and confidently that God would be honored and that others would feel valued and cared for because of my questions. That my faith and the faith of others would be deepened because of them. And that creative ideas would flow and new ways of thinking would emerge. *If the quality of our lives is directly linked to the quality of the questions we ask of God, ourselves, and others, why would we not ask God to give us the ability to ask better ones?*

ASK QUESTIONS, BUT KNOW WHEN TO STOP

Questions are immensely valuable, but that doesn't mean we should use them all the time. While focusing on growing in our questions is great, we can't simply sit around and ask questions all day. In fact, too many questions can be exhausting, frustrating, and unhelpful for both you and others. I've seen well-intentioned people desire to improve in their ability, but they inadvertently develop an extreme case of obsessive tunnel vision. It's all they can think about, and it can annoy the snot out of people. There are times where we need to stop asking questions and act. Or sit in silence and reflect. Knowing when to ask questions—and when it's time to stop—is crucial to the process.

ONE LAST STEP

Whether we're learning to play an instrument or speaking a new language, we only get better when we engage in focused and frequent practice. It's no different with questions. As you begin, you won't be able to use questions pyrotechnically, but you have to start somewhere. Nobody becomes Oprah overnight, not even Oprah. Flip through the last three chapters and review the practices. Then identify just *one or two practices or action steps* you can take in each of the three categories. Circle them or draw a star next to them. Write them down in the blank pages in the back, commit to experimenting with them within the next two weeks, and see what happens. Again, there are numerous resources in the back of the book to help you.

Conclusion

NOW WHAT?

In the word question, *there is a beautiful word—*quest.
I love that word.

ELIE WIESEL

*I want to beg you, as much as I can, dear sir, to be patient toward
all that is unsolved in your heart and to try to love the questions
themselves like locked rooms and like books that are written
in a very foreign tongue. Do not now seek the answers,
which cannot be given to you because you would not be able to
live them. And the point is, to live everything. Live the questions
now. Perhaps you will then gradually, without noticing
it, live along some distant day into the answer.*

RAINER MARIA RILKE

SEVERAL YEARS AGO, I was leading an all-day training event
for leaders gathered from around the state of Florida who wanted
to learn how to ask better questions. I was pouring my heart and soul
into the presentation, and people were following along, laughing at my
jokes, engaging in conversation, and writing down notes. But not everyone. There was one guy in the back of the room who clearly wasn't

convinced. He leaned back in his chair with his arms folded and chewed his gum slowly. He took no notes the entire day. In fact, he had nothing on the table in front of him but a half-finished bottle of Dr Pepper. Several times during the presentation, I glanced back at him to see if anything was getting through to this guy. I kept noticing how often he would stare out the window, probably daydreaming about the many other ways he'd rather be spending a beautiful Saturday in March than sitting in that room.

Though others were engaged, I couldn't stop thinking about the guy in the back row. *Why can't I get through to him? What's his deal? Why did he even show up today?* He was utterly uninterested and completely checked out. I'd had wonderful interactions with several participants during the breaks sprinkled throughout the day. They asked thoughtful follow-up questions, and we engaged in meaningful interactions. Together we had brainstormed questions they could ask among their families, friends, and colleagues. But I just couldn't shake my thoughts about the guy in the back row. At the end of the day, I thanked the room and dismissed them—and then made a beeline for Back Row Guy.

I shook his hand, and he told me his name was Mason.

"You're not buying any of this stuff about questions, are you?" I said with a smile.

Caught a bit off guard, he laughed nervously and admitted, "No, I guess not."

I told Mason that was fine and assured him my job wasn't to twist his arm to do something he didn't seem to care much about. I wasn't offended, but I was curious. "Why not?"

"I'm just not convinced that questions can be as powerful and as helpful as you say they are."

"Okay. I appreciate your honesty," I conceded, "but can I offer you a challenge, Mason?"

"Sure. Whatcha got?" His body language told me loud and clear that, while he was polite, he clearly wasn't thrilled with the suggestion.

"For the next seven days, I want you to play a game nobody else knows you're playing. I want you to try to be the most curious person you can possibly be. Ask a few more questions than you normally do—and ask them with just a little more thought and intention than you have in the past. That's it. Don't do anything else. And then just see what happens."

He smirked, shook my hand silently, and quickly walked away. I collected my bag and headed to my rental car. *That guy will never do it.*

About ten months later, I was speaking at another event in the Midwest. When my talk concluded, I walked off the platform and was met immediately by a guy flashing a big smile. "Remember me?" he asked.

It took me a moment, but then I remembered: it was Mason, Back Row Guy. But his demeanor was different from our last interaction. With excitement in his voice, Mason told me that he had driven away from the training and thought, *What the heck—why not? I'll give that challenge a try.* On his way home, he brainstormed a few interesting questions he might ask his wife, the kinds of questions he used to ask back when they were dating but hadn't asked in who knows how long. He also thought about a few he might want to ask his two daughters. He sent himself a voice memo with a few ideas so he wouldn't forget.

At work the following week, he thought about the sales team at the small company where he worked, especially the weekly Tuesday-morning team meetings led by his boss, which were irrelevant and a significant waste of time. He wondered if he could make them a bit more interesting and helpful if he asked two or three questions regarding their products and the vendors they worked with. Mason shared that he did the same thing with his coworkers during lunch and his golf buddies during their next round. He began asking follow-up questions. And a few more. And a few more. He found himself in new and interesting conversations he hadn't experienced since college.

As he continued to share, he got even more excited. He told me others also began to ask him interesting and meaningful questions.

Over the past few months, he'd laughed, told stories, and even choked up in his interactions more than he had in years. He felt closer to his daughters than ever before, remaining immensely curious while getting down on the floor and playing with their dolls.

Then Mason's voice cracked as he shared what had happened just two weeks prior. During an interesting and engaging conversation with his wife in the kitchen, she had paused midsentence, looked at him with a beautiful smile and soft eyes, and said, "You've changed. I don't know what has happened, but you've changed. I feel deeply loved by the questions you're asking me."

Now, blinking away tears, he said all he'd done was take me up on the challenge—not for just a week but for the past several months. "I wasn't convinced before, but I am now," he said. "Questions work. Life's better because of questions."

Life *is* better because of questions. They are some of the most valuable and easily accessible tools available to every one of us. When we make a commitment to learn to ask better questions, we experience better marriages and families, cultivate closer friendships, and deepen our faith. We have the opportunity to humanize our places of work, build stronger schools, and create more connected neighborhoods. Learn to see the world as a question mark, and the journey never ends.

If the quality of your life is determined by the quality of the questions you ask God, yourself, and others, how then will you live into those questions?

ACKNOWLEDGMENTS

THERE'S A PICTURE FRAME that sits on my desk, just to the right of my computer monitor, that holds an old black-and-white photograph of the writer E. B. White. He's sitting by himself in a primitive boathouse with his fingers gently resting on the keys of a typewriter that sits on a simple wooden table. The photo serves as a constant reminder that I must put my butt in the seat and get to work, because books don't just write themselves. This image kept me focused during the writing process.

But that's only half the story. Most often, when writers craft a book, there's a group of selfless servants who are just out of view yet standing close by. They are supportive, encouraging and challenging the writer to keep going. Along the way, they serve as conversation partners, offering constructive feedback, giving helpful perspective, and pushing the writer to make words march in synchronous formation.

I'm deeply grateful for a team of people who, over the past several months (and in some cases, years), have been those literary cheerleaders and conversation partners just slightly out of the picture frame. These people have helped me to steward the message of this book from start to finish, and they deserve mention for their labor of love: Lila Stoeckle, Stephen Redden, Tom Kang, Melissa Sievers, Caleb Mangum, Jennifer Jukanovich, Matt Lake, Dave Bielecki, Tom Smith, Rita Platt, Chad Eigsti, Christina (Chris) Jackson, Janet Durrwachter, Wes Tillett, Megan Monterrosa, Jeremiah Link, Maria Metzler, Mike Candy, Jerry Heslinga, Linda Hannigan, Michael Kaspar, Anthony

Hamilton, Bradley Rikard, Brandon Hanks, Audrey Reeves, Bryan Scott, Candy Nixon, Chad Stewart, Charles Brodany, Chris Stroup, Colin McKay Miller, Michelle Christian Curtis, Mike Ford, Mitchell Lavender, Kristen Curtis, Nathan Armstrong, Rich Morey, Roger Vest, Tim Knight, Gino Curcuruto, Dennis Chachko, Gary Richardson, Graham Rider, Janet Crow, Joel Knox, Johnny Douglas, Jonathan Gordon, Kaitlin Neel, Katie Lukashow, Kelly Raudenbush, Kira Mitchell, Jim Thomas, Jacob Vangen, Peter Englert, Todd Willard, Kristina Meece, Lisa Hadja, Luke Maggard, Michael Smith, Dave Briggs, Brandon Morrow, Tim Knipp, Justin Copenhaver, and Ryan McKenzie. Three additional folks deserve special recognition: Jared Mackey, Scott Bolinder, and Eddy Hall went above and beyond, eagerly providing valuable, thorough, and thoughtful feedback on numerous occasions.

To Dr. Derek Cooper, who agreed to serve as my adviser in the Doctor of Ministry program at Missio Seminary on one condition: that I research and write on the topic of teaching leaders how to ask better questions. He knew this was my passion, and he knew there was a book in there somewhere. Because of this, he gave me the permission to study and write toward that end. This book would not be what it is without his vision, encouragement, and feedback throughout my academic journey.

To Michael Smith, who cowrote and illustrated a small, limited-edition book with me several years ago on question-asking that also helped to plant some early seeds for the development of this book.

To my oldest son, Carter, who helped with numerous research details—finding original sources and formatting footnotes—throughout the writing and editing process.

To my Kairos Partnerships team. It continues to be an immense joy to serve alongside you as we care for, equip, and help leaders overcome their unique challenges so they can thrive in their calling. I love doing this with you.

To the many friends, leaders, and event hosts who over the years have invited me to speak on this topic. These spaces helped me to learn from you and refine this message even more.

To my agent, Don Pape, who I've known for more than half my lifetime. I've appreciated your constant encouragement, insight, and perspective throughout the years, especially with this project.

To my editor, Al Hsu, who continually pushed me to be a clearer and more streamlined writer. This book is better because of your keen insight and gentle touch. Thanks for taking on another project with me. You are one of the best in the business.

To the InterVarsity Press team. I'm deeply honored and thankful to partner with you all once again. I continue to be grateful for the healthy balance you possess with excellence in publishing and a warm personal touch.

And to Megan, Carter, and Bennett for extending grace and patience to me well beyond what I deserve. I'm so glad we are a family.

RESOURCES

DISCUSSION GUIDE

1. What portion(s) of the book did you find most helpful? Interesting? Provocative?
2. Several questions were italicized throughout the book. Were there any specific italicized questions you found beneficial or memorable? Why those?
3. How do you view questions and question-asking now compared to before you began reading the book? How has your perspective changed?
4. Were there any elements in the book that you disagree with? If so, what were they? Is there anything the author left out that you wish he had included?
5. What story or stories from the book remain with you? Do you have your own story to share of a time you asked or were asked a powerful question?
6. Who are the people in your life who ask great questions? What makes them, in the words of David Brooks, Illuminators?
7. There are many barriers that can keep us from asking better questions. What do you believe are the biggest barriers for you?
8. The introduction notes, "We don't have a shortage of information; we have a shortage of wisdom, curiosity, and wonder." What implications might that have for us today? For you?

9. Chapter two says there are four essentials to asking great questions: curiosity, wisdom, humility, and courage. In which of these four areas do you believe you are doing well? What is one area where you believe you need to grow the most?

10. Think about the four levels of good questions mentioned in chapter three. Can you name two or three of the best questions you have asked or you've been asked on each level?

11. Think about the concept of shift-response versus support-response (chapter three). Can you think of a time where you or others were engaged in either of these responses? Now that you are aware of this dynamic, how might this help you in future conversations?

12. Were you surprised to learn that Jesus asked more than three hundred questions in the Gospels? Were you surprised to learn that out of the more than 180 questions he was asked, he only directly answered five of them? (See Resource 4.) Why or why not?

13. Of the recorded questions Jesus asked in the New Testament, which are your favorites?

14. How does Jesus' willingness to ask questions frequently affect how you think about and interact with him?

15. Chapter nine explores the Jewish Scripture-reading practice called *chavruta*, which involves reading a passage and asking a series of questions about the text. Have you ever engaged in this practice before? If so, how did you experience it? If you're considering engaging with it, how might implementing this practice—either in your own life or with others—help you engage with Scripture more fully and with God more deeply?

16. Chapter nine concludes, "We don't stunt our spiritual formation by asking questions. We stunt our formation when we don't." How does this strike you? How can asking better questions help

shape your own spiritual formation? How might it help shape other people's formation?

17. What questions do you most frequently ask of God? What questions might you want or need to ask God more frequently? Why those?

18. What questions has God asked you? What have you done or what will you do with those questions?

19. After reading a book geared toward asking better questions, did you find yourself asking new or different questions than you have in the past? If so, what were they?

20. If you could ask the author one or two questions, what would you want to ask him?

21. If your ability to ask better questions never grew from what it is today, what impact might that have on you and others?

22. If your ability to ask better questions were to improve moving forward, what impact might that have on you and others?

23. If you are to grow in asking better questions by just 5 or 10 percent, what would need to happen?

24. Of the practical next steps listed in chapters eleven through thirteen, what two or three did you find most helpful?

25. If someone asked you to help them become a better question-asker, how would you go about trying to help them—and where would you start?

26. So . . . now what?

Resource 2

QUESTIONS TO ASK OURSELVES

SELF-REFLECTION QUESTIONS

- Who am I, and why am I here?
- When was I least energized in the past few months? When was I most energized?
- What's on my to-do list?
- What's on my to-don't list?
- What were my top three highlights from this past week/month/quarter/year?
- What were my three most significant low points?
- What are my top three to five core values that define and guide my life? Does my lifestyle align with those values?
- What or who do I need to appreciate or celebrate?
- What mistakes have I made, and what lessons have I learned from them? Which one is my favorite mistake?
- Who helped, supported, and encouraged me the most the past few months? How can I thank them?
- Who could I help, support, and encourage this month?
- How am I different now than I was a year ago?
- Who do I want to become a year from now, and what will it take to get me there?

- What are the brutal facts about my life that I need to name, face, and embrace?
- What were the main factors that got in the way of my growth this year?
- What are my unique opportunities and limitations in this season?
- What was the most beautiful or inspiring thing I've seen or experienced in the past month?
- Positive or negative, which words from my interactions with others carry the most significance for me? Why those?
- What are two things I would change if I had enough courage to attempt it?
- How do fear, anxiety, and worry affect my relationships?
- Who can journey with me in this season of my life, and how would I want them to join me on the journey?
- If I had to pick between being smart or being wise, which would I choose? Why?
- Which projects, initiatives, and people should have my time, energy, focus, and attention in this season? Why those?
- What will I need to say no to in this season—even if they are good things—to accomplish my goals?
- Where do I need to extend grace and mercy to others? To myself?
- What does a well-rested me look and feel like? Where will there be spaces for me to rest, recreate, and replenish in solitude? With others?
- What is *most essential* that I need to focus on in this season of my life?
- What risks do I believe I need to take this year? Why those?
- What's the next best thing for me to do moving forward?
- What is worth knowing? Feeling? Doing? Refraining from doing?
- What do I need to learn? Unlearn? Relearn?

- What is in my control and what is out of my control in this situation?

SPIRITUALLY ORIENTED REFLECTION QUESTIONS

- Where has God been present in my life in the past few months? Where do I long for God to work in my life? Where do I long for God to work in my community and context?
- Where is conversion needed in my life?
- If God had his way in my life, what would it look like in ten years? Next month? Tomorrow?
- Where have I sensed God's presence most strongly in the past week/month?
- What season am I currently in?
- What three adjectives would I use to describe the current state of my soul?
- How can I grow to become a more cooperative friend of Jesus?
- Is it well with my soul?
- Which relationships in my life need repair? What part will I play to work toward repair? When will I do it?
- If Jesus is King, how then should I live?

SELF-REFLECTION QUESTIONS FOR LEADERS

- What gives me the right to lead others?
- Because I have power and authority, who, in turn, is now flourishing because of it?
- Am I a leader who serves or a servant who leads? How would I know the difference?
- Leadership is an intentional decision of choosing who to disappoint. So, who will I choose to disappoint in this season? And who do I need to work hard for to ensure I do not disappoint?

- Where have I failed in my leadership, and what have I learned from it? Do I need to apologize to anyone for my failures?
- What can I celebrate in my leadership?
- Who should I invest in?
- How can I stay sharp in this season?
- Who leads me? Who will I follow?
- What if we rewarded boldly asked questions just as much as, if not more than, accurately articulated answers? What if we deemphasized monologue to more rightly emphasize dialogue?
- Instead of our organization prioritizing a purpose statement, what if we developed purpose questions? What would some of those purpose questions be?
- As a leader, where and how do I need to get out of my own way?
- Where do I need to be more involved with those I lead? Where do I need to get out of the way of others so they can thrive?
- Who in my life has the authority to say no to me?
- What are the primary questions I'm asking of myself in this season of my leadership?
- Am I a leader trying to love God or a lover of God trying to lead?

PERSONAL-FEEDBACK QUESTIONS

Ask five to eight of your trusted friends, colleagues, and family members to give you honest feedback for the following questions.

- What would you say are my greatest strengths? What do I do exceptionally well with minimal effort?
- When do you believe I am most alive? What activities am I doing? Who am I with? What situations am I in when you notice this?
- What do you believe are the areas where I need to grow the most?
- From a relational perspective, do you believe I am functioning in my sweet spot?

- From a vocational perspective, do you think I am functioning in my sweet spot? What potential adjustments might I need to make to live and lead more in my sweet spot?
- What is it like to be on the other side of me?
- What am I like when I'm under stress?
- What concerns or hesitancies do you have about me and my future?
- What does a healthy me look like?
- As you think about my life and future, what do you want to say to me?

GORDON MacDONALD'S QUESTIONS IN DIFFERENT DECADES OF YOUR LIFE

The questions of your twenties: Life is marked by optimism, opportunities, and potential. It's an exciting time filled with possibility as we look forward. This is a decade of discovery and expectancy where hope and energy are high.

1. What kind of man or woman am I becoming?
2. How am I different from my mother or father?
3. Where can I find a few friends who will welcome me as I am and who will offer the family-like connections that I need (or never had)?
4. Can I love, and am I lovable?
5. What will I do with my life?
6. What do I really want in exchange for my life's labors?
7. What parts of me need correction?
8. Around what person or conviction will I organize my life?

The questions of your thirties: Spiritual life changes in our thirties. Our spiritual questions no longer center on the ideals of our youth but on the reality that life is tough and unforgiving. Thirty-somethings likely see things in themselves they thought they might have overcome by now simply by growing up.

1. How do I prioritize the demands being made on my life?
2. How far can I go in fulfilling my sense of purpose?
3. Where are the people I know I can walk through life with?
4. What does my spiritual life look like? Do I even have time for one?
5. Why am I not a better person?

The questions of your forties: The complexities of life further accelerate, and we begin to recognize we can no longer shrug off our flaws and failures as youthfulness and inexperience. We're grownups now, expected to handle the bumps and bruises of life with unshakable courage. We are expected to be solid, yet if we listen carefully, we might hear the word *trapped* in the questions that now rise within us.

1. Who was I as a child, and what powers back then influenced the person I am today?
2. Why do some people seem to be doing better than I am?
3. Why am I often disappointed in myself and others?
4. Why are limitations beginning to outnumber options?
5. Why do I seem to face so many uncertainties?
6. What can I do to make a greater contribution to my generation? Or what would it take to pick up a whole new calling in life and do this thing I've always wanted to do?

The questions of your fifties: We prefer not to think about it, but we have moved across life's middle. Now we wonder how many years we have left. This is a decade of friends dying, marriages dissolving, and people moving to places of retirement. It can be sobering—even frightening—when we discover that younger people may know more than us.

1. Why is time moving so fast?
2. Why is my body becoming unreliable?

3. How do I deal with my failures and my successes?

4. How can my spouse and I reinvigorate our relationship now that our kids are gone?

5. Who are these young people who want to replace me?

6. What do I do with my doubts and fears?

7. Will I have enough money for my retirement years if I experience health problems and economic downturns?

The questions of your sixties:

1. When do I stop doing the things that have always defined me?

2. Why do I feel ignored by a large part of the younger population?

3. Why am I curious about who is listed in the obituary column of the papers, how they died, and what kinds of lives they led?

4. Do I have enough time to do all the things I've dreamed about in the past?

5. Who will be around me when I die?

6. If I'm married, which one of us will go first? What is it like to say goodbye to someone with whom you've shared so many years of life?

7. Are the things I believe in capable of taking me to the end?

8. Is there really life after death?

9. What do I regret?

10. What are the chief satisfactions of this many years of living?

11. What have I done that will outlive me?

The questions of your seventies and eighties: The questions of these decades blend together and share similarities.

1. Does anyone realize or even care who I once was?

2. Is anyone aware that I once owned or managed a business, threw a mean curveball, possessed a beautiful solo voice, or had an attractive face?

3. Is my story important to anyone?

4. How much of my life can I still control?

5. Is there anything I can still contribute?

6. Why am I experiencing this anger and irritability?

7. Is God really there for me?

8. Am I ready to face death?

9. When I die, how will it happen? Will I be missed, or will the news of my death bring relief?

10. What is heaven like?

DISCUSSION QUESTIONS FOR FAITH COMMUNITIES

- What is Jesus currently doing in our context?
- What is the Spirit's intent with our church? How can we join the Spirit in that?
- How can we move toward strategic uncertainty?
- If the kingdom of God were fully realized in our city or region, what would that look like in ten years? Next month? What would that require of us?
- As the adage goes, "What you celebrate is what you care about." What do we celebrate? What do we need to celebrate more? What do we need to celebrate less?
- If you knew it would not fail, what would you do for the glory of God and the growth of his kingdom?
- Are we striving to grow a spiritual organism or build a religious machine? How would we know?
- What is our plan for discipleship in our church? Does it work?
- If we did nothing different from what we are doing right now, what might our church look like in fifty years? Are we encouraged about that prospect?
- Is our core vision worth dying for?

- How can we cultivate a culture in which people expect God to be active in their everyday lives?
- What would our church look like if together we all sought first the kingdom of God (Mt 6:33)?
- What do we need to grieve and mourn?
- What stories need to be told more often?
- How can we help people fall more in love with Christ?
- If we focused more on growing hearts than on growing numbers, what would we do differently? Is it worth it?
- What do the prayers of our church currently center around? What are the prominent themes in them? What does that say about us as a faith community?
- What is the glue that holds our church together?

FASCINATING FACTS ABOUT THE QUESTIONS JESUS ASKED

JESUS WAS ASKED MORE than one hundred eighty questions, but he only answered five of them directly—and four semidirectly.

FIVE DIRECT ANSWERS

Matthew 17:19-20 (healing): "Then the disciples came to Jesus in private and asked, 'Why couldn't we drive it out?' He replied, 'Because you have so little faith.'"

Matthew 18:21-22 (forgiveness): "Then Peter came to Jesus and asked, 'Lord, how many times shall I forgive my brother or sister who sins against me? Up to seven times?' Jesus answered, 'I tell you, not seven times, but seventy-seven times.'"

Mark 12:28-31 (the greatest commandment): "One of the teachers of the law came and heard them debating. Noticing that Jesus had given them a good answer, he asked him, 'Of all the commandments, which is the most important?'

"'The most important one,' answered Jesus, 'is this: 'Hear, O Israel: The Lord our God, the Lord is one. Love the Lord your God with all your heart and with all your soul and with all your mind and with all your strength.' The second is this: 'Love your neighbor as yourself.' There is no commandment greater than these.'"

Matthew 19:20-21 (rich young ruler): "'All these I have kept,' the young man said. 'What do I still lack?' Jesus answered, 'If you want to

be perfect, go, sell your possessions and give to the poor, and you will
have treasure in heaven. Then come, follow me.'"

Mark 14:61-62 (Jesus' identity): "Again the high priest asked him,
'Are you the Messiah, the Son of the Blessed One?'

"'I am,' said Jesus. 'And you will see the Son of Man sitting at the right
hand of the Mighty One and coming on the clouds of heaven.'"

FOUR SEMIDIRECT ANSWERS

Matthew 19:3-9 (interpretation of the law): "Some Pharisees came to
him to test him. They asked, 'Is it lawful for a man to divorce his wife
for any and every reason?'

"'Haven't you read,' he replied, 'that at the beginning the Creator
'made them male and female,' and said, 'For this reason a man will leave
his father and mother and be united to his wife, and the two will
become one flesh'? So they are no longer two, but one flesh. Therefore
what God has joined together, let no one separate.'

"'Why then,' they asked, 'did Moses command that a man give his
wife a certificate of divorce and send her away?'

"Jesus replied, 'Moses permitted you to divorce your wives because
your hearts were hard. But it was not this way from the beginning. I tell
you that anyone who divorces his wife, except for sexual immorality,
and marries another woman commits adultery.'"

Mark 14:12-15 (instructions on the Passover meal): "On the first
day of the Festival of Unleavened Bread, when it was customary to
sacrifice the Passover lamb, Jesus' disciples asked him, 'Where do you
want us to go and make preparations for you to eat the Passover?'

"So he sent two of his disciples, telling them, 'Go into the city, and
a man carrying a jar of water will meet you. Follow him. Say to the
owner of the house he enters, "The Teacher asks: Where is my guest
room, where I may eat the Passover with my disciples?" He will show
you a large room upstairs, furnished and ready. Make preparations for
us there.'"

Luke 23:3 (Jesus' identity): "So Pilate asked Jesus, 'Are you the king of the Jews?'

"'You have said so,' Jesus replied."

John 13:21-30 (the betrayer at the table): "After he had said this, Jesus was troubled in spirit and testified, 'Very truly I tell you, one of you is going to betray me.'

"His disciples stared at one another, at a loss to know which of them he meant. One of them, the disciple whom Jesus loved, was reclining next to him. Simon Peter motioned to this disciple and said, 'Ask him which one he means.'

"Leaning back against Jesus, he asked him, 'Lord, who is it?'

"Jesus answered, 'It is the one to whom I will give this piece of bread when I have dipped it in the dish.' Then, dipping the piece of bread, he gave it to Judas, the son of Simon Iscariot. As soon as Judas took the bread, Satan entered into him.

"So Jesus told him, 'What you are about to do, do quickly.' But no one at the meal understood why Jesus said this to him. Since Judas had charge of the money, some thought Jesus was telling him to buy what was needed for the festival, or to give something to the poor. As soon as Judas had taken the bread, he went out. And it was night."

JESUS' MOST REPEATED QUESTIONS

- "Haven't you read?" (Mt 12:3, 5; 19:4; 22:31; Mk 12:10, 26)
- "What do you want me to do for you?" (Mt 20:32; Mk 10:36, 51; Lk 18:41)
- "What do you think?" (Mt 18:12; 21:28; 22:42; 26:66)

THE SEVEN MAJOR THEMES OF JESUS' QUESTIONS

1. Sabbath law interpretation
2. Worry (six in the Sermon on the Mount)
3. Understanding/knowing
4. Evil spirits and demonic activity

5. His authority and identity

6. Interpretation of Scripture

7. Faith, unbelief, and doubt: Jesus often asked jolting rhetorical questions such as, "Why do you doubt?" and ended questions with " . . . you of little faith."

- He asked why the disciples possessed such little faith (Mt 6:30; 8:26; 16:8), why they doubted (Mt 14:31; Lk 24:38), and why they were so dull (Mt 15:16; Mk 7:18).

- He questioned their understanding (Mt 16:9, 11; Mk 4:13-14; 8:17; Jn 13:12).

- All three Synoptic Gospels record Jesus asking how long he should stay with this unbelieving generation (Mt 17:17; Mk 9:19; Lk 9:41).

WHO JESUS DIRECTED HIS QUESTIONS TO

Jesus asked questions of all sorts of people, but the bulk of his questions were directed at three distinct groups: his disciples, the crowds, and the religious experts. But other groups included:

- Rich and poor
- Men and women—he asked questions of seven women: his mother, the mother of Zebedee's children, the woman subject to bleeding, the woman at the well, the woman caught in adultery, Martha (the brother of Lazarus), and Mary (at the tomb).
- Jews and Gentiles
- Religious and irreligious
- Friends and enemies
- Sick and healthy
- Those at the center of power and those on the margins

WHERE JESUS ASKED HIS QUESTIONS

The Gospels record that Jesus asked questions in at least twenty-seven different locations, but there are also instances where the location is unknown or unnamed.

- *Towns and villages:* Capernaum, towns around Galilee, Caesarea Philippi, Jericho, Bethsaida, Cana, Bethany, and Jerusalem
- *Regions:* between Samaria and Galilee, Greek territory on the east side of the Sea of Galilee, and Judea on the other side of the Jordan
- *Indoors:* the synagogue, the upper room, the palace in Jerusalem, and the houses of lepers, tax collectors, and synagogue rulers
- *Outdoors:* mountains, the Sea of Galilee, fields, temple courts, a garden, the wilderness, a wedding (presumably outdoors), a well, a pool, on the cross, near the tomb, on the road, on the shore of the Sea of Galilee, and in a boat on the lake

NOTES

INTRODUCTION: WHY DO WE ASK QUESTIONS?

3   *Albert Einstein asked himself:* Abraham Pais, *Subtle is the Lord: The Science and the Life of Albert Einstein* (Oxford: Oxford University Press, 1982).

4   *What are you doing for others:* Rev. Dr. Martin Luther King Jr. delivered this line during a sermon at Dexter Avenue Baptist Church in Montgomery, Alabama, on August 11, 1957.

5   *People who ask frequent questions:* The University of Utah, the University of Pennsylvania, and Emory University to name a few.

     They have more social influence: Charles Duhigg, *Supercommunicators: How to Unlock the Secret Language of Connection* (New York: Random House, 2024), 101.

     Asking better questions helps: Joseph Grenny, Kerry Patterson, Ron McMillan, Al Switzler, and Emily Gregory, *Crucial Conversations: Tools for Talking When the Stakes Are High,* 3rd ed. (New York: McGraw Hill, 2021).

     More effective reading comprehension: Shane Parrish, "The Art of Reading: How to be a Demanding Reader," *Farnham Street*, www.fs.blog/the-art-of-reading-how-to-be-a-demanding-reader; Mary Ann Corley and W. Christiane Rauscher, "TEAL Center Fact Sheet No. 12: Deeper Learning Through Questioning," Teaching Excellence in Adult Literacy, 2013, https://lincs.ed.gov/sites/default/files/12_TEAL_Deeper_Learning_Qs_complete_5_1_0.pdf.

     Questions stimulate your brain: Neil Cooper, "What Effect Do Questions Have On Our Brain?," *Medium*, March 15, 2018, www.medium.com/@mr.neilcooper/what-effect-do-questions-have-on-our-brain-329c37d69948.

     A reflex called instinctive elaboration: David Hoffeld, "What Does the Brain Do When It Hears a Question?," CAIL, November 30, 2021, www.cail.com/business-innovation/what-does-the-brain-do-when-it-hears-a-question.

6   *While most of us believe:* Paul Atchley, "You Can't Multitask, So Stop Trying,"
    Harvard Business Review, December 21, 2010, www.hbr.org/2010/12/you
    -cant-multi-task-so-stop-tr.

    Raise your Question/Answer ratio: A phrase I first read in Jeff Dyer, Hal Gre-
    gersen, and Clayton M. Christensen, *The Innovator's DNA: Mastering the Five
    Skills of Disruptive Innovators* (Boston: Harvard Business Review Press,
    2019), 23.

8   *They are archaeologists' tools:* Warren Berger, *A More Beautiful Question: The
    Power of Inquiry to Spark Breakthrough Ideas* (New York: Bloomsbury,
    2014), 15.

    Good questions are flashlights: Dan Rothstein and Luz Santana, *Make Just One
    Change: Teach Students to Ask Their Own Questions* (Cambridge: Harvard Edu-
    cation Press, 2012), 37.

    They are screwdrivers that: Fran Peavey, *By Life's Grace: Musings on the Essence
    of Social Change* (Gabriola Island, BC, Canada: New Society Publishers,
    1994), 23.

12 *In every crowd there are:* David Brooks, *How to Know a Person: The Art of Seeing
    Others Deeply and Being Deeply Seen* (New York: Random House, 2023), 12-13.

1. WHY OUR APPROACH TO QUESTIONS NEEDS TO CHANGE

14 *Each robe and hood: Accidental Courtesy: Daryl Davis, Race & America*,
    directed by Matthew Ornstein (2016, Sound & Vision Productions, 2016),
    documentary.

    His dream is to: Dwane Brown, "How One Man Convinced 200 Ku Klux Klan
    Members to Give Up Their Robes," *NPR*, August 20, 2017, www.npr
    .org/2017/08/20/544861933/how-one-man-convinced-200-ku-klux-klan
    -members-to-give-up-their-robes.

    That simple yet piercing question: I've shared Daryl Davis's story before in my
    previous book, *The Sacred Overlap*. Because it's so powerful, it bears re-
    peating here.

    Held in high esteem: Edgar H. Schein and Peter A. Schein, *Humble Inquiry: The
    Gentle Art of Asking Instead of Telling*, 2nd ed., rev. and exp. (Oakland, CA:
    Barrett-Koehler Publishers, 2021), 71.

15 *I can only answer the question:* Alasdair MacIntyre, *After Virtue: A Study in
    Moral Theory,* (Notre Dame, IN: University of Notre Dame, 1981), 216.

16 *A list of thirty-six questions:* Kelly Gonsalves, "The 36 Questions to Fall in Love:
    The Research Behind the Viral Experiment," *mindbodygreen*, January 12, 2024,
    www.mindbodygreen.com/articles/36-questions-to-fall-in-love.

16   *The Arons' research was popularized:* Mandy Len Catron, "To Fall in Love with Anyone, Do This," *New York Times*, January 9, 2015, www.nytimes.com /2015/01/11/style/modern-love-to-fall-in-love-with-anyone-do-this.html.

How would I respond: Martin B. Copenhaver, *Jesus Is the Question: The 307 Questions Jesus Asked and the 3 He Answered* (Nashville, TN: Abingdon, 2014), 49.

17   *They, quite literally, have fresh eyes:* Warren Berger, *A More Beautiful Question: The Power of Inquiry to Spark Breakthrough Ideas* (New York: Bloomsbury, 2014), 43.

The average child asks: Will Storr, *The Science of Storytelling: Why Stories Make Us Human and How to Tell Them Better* (New York: Abrams, 2020), 17.

By their fourth birthday: Storr, *Science of Storytelling*, 40.

The average four-year-old girl: "Mothers Asked Nearly 300 Questions a Day, Study Finds," *Telegraph*, March 28, 2013, www.telegraph.co.uk/news /uknews/9959026/Mothers-asked-nearly-300-questions-a-day-study-finds .html.

Completely ceased asking questions: Brandon Busteed, "The School Cliff: Student Engagement Drops with Each School Year," School Leadership 2.0, January 15, 2013, https://schoolleadership20.com/forum/topics/the-school -cliff-student-engagement-drops-with-each-school-year.

18   *Seldom is permission given:* Dennis Palmer Wolf, "The Art of Questioning" (lecture, Summer Institute of College Boards of Educational Equality Project, Santa Cruz, CA, July 12, 1986).

Is it not curious, then: Neil Postman, *Building a Bridge to the 18th Century: How the Past Can Improve Our Future* (New York: Random House, 1999), 171.

This is why students: Postman, *Building a Bridge*.

The priority should not be: Abraham Joshua Heschel, *The Insecurity of Freedom: Essays on Human Existence* (New York: Schocken Books, 1972), 46-47.

Rephrase the ancient Chinese proverb: Heschel, *Insecurity of Freedom*, 47.

19   *Well-known graduates of:* Peter Sims, *Little Bets: How Breakthrough Ideas Emerge from Small Discoveries* (New York: Simon & Schuster, 2013), 115.

Bezos believes so strongly: David Ayer, "Amazon's Jeff Bezos Pledges Billions for Montessori (Inspired)," *MontessoriPublic*, National Center for Montessori in the Public Sector, October 1, 2018, www.montessoripublic.org/2018/10 /amazons-jeff-bezos-pledges-blllions-for-montessori-inspired/.

For founder Maria Montessori: Berger, *A More Beautiful Question*, 49.

19   *Leaders at the Right Question Institute:* Right Question Institute, www.right question.org.

19   *Question Formulation Technique:* Dan Rothstein and Luz Santana, *Make Just One Change: Teach Students to Ask Their Own Questions* (Cambridge, MA: Harvard Education Press, 2011), 25-26.

20   *The world is so complicated:* Kate Zernike, "Tests Are Not Just for Kids," *New York Times*, August 4, 2002, www.nytimes.com/2002/08/04/education/tests -are-not-just-for-kids.html.
      When we're thinking about ourselves: Charles Derber, *The Pursuit of Attention: Power and Ego in Everyday Life* (New York: Oxford University Press, 2000), 19.
      Jordan was my favorite: As great as LeBron James is, I stand by my conviction: Jordan is the greatest player to ever play the game.

21   *Two wonderfully helpful books:* See Warren Berger, *A More Beautiful Question* (New York: Bloomsbury Publishing, 2014) and Warren Berger, *The Book of Beautiful Questions* (New York: Bloomsbury Publishing, 2018).
      Ray Dalio, founder of: Amy Edmondson, *Right Kind of Wrong: The Science of Failing Well* (New York: Atria Books, 2023), 168.
      The truth is we don't know: Berger, *The Book of Beautiful Questions*, 10.

22   *The illiterate of the 21st century:* Alvin Toffler, *Future Shock* (New York: Bantam Books, 1970), 23.
      These places are called: Clayton M. Christensen, *The Innovator's Dilemma: The Revolutionary Book That Will Change the Way You Do Business* (New York: Harper Business, 2011), 39.

23   *But if we can build:* Michael Bungay Stanier, *The Advice Trap: Be Humble, Stay Curious, and Change the Way You Lead Forever* (Toronto: Box of Crayons Press, 2020), 1.
      Can lead to hatred and violence: Mark Matlock, *Faith for the Curious: How an Era of Spiritual Openness Shapes the Way We Live and Help Others Follow Jesus* (Grand Rapids, MI: Baker Books, 2024), 104.
      Our world is insecure: David Brooks, *How to Know a Person: The Art of Seeing Others Deeply and Being Deeply Seen* (New York: Random House, 2023), 85.
      Asking questions can even be hazardous: Jeff Dyer, Hal Gregersen, and Clayton M. Christensen, *The Innovator's DNA: Mastering the Five Skills of Disruptive Innovators* (Boston: Harvard Business Review Press, 2019), 5.
      Sometimes the only way: Dyer, Gregersen, and Christensen, *The Innovator's DNA*, 29.

24   *Listen, listen, listen, listen:* Brooks, *How to Know a Person*, 93.
      Neurologist John Kounios: Berger, *A More Beautiful Question*, 6.
      Often operate on autopilot: Lorraine Daston and Katharine Park, *Wonders and the Order of Nature* (New York: Zone Books, 1998), 122.

2. THE POWER AND POSSIBILITY OF QUESTIONS

27   *By then it was obvious:* Parker J. Palmer, *Let Your Life Speak: Listening for the Voice of Vocation* (New York: Jossey-Bass, 2000), 44-46.

28   *Right question to reframe their problem:* Jeff Dyer, Hal Gregersen, and Clayton M. Christensen, *The Innovator's DNA: Mastering the Five Skills of Disruptive Innovators* (Boston: Harvard Business Review Press, 2019), 70.

     Maltese physician Edward de Bono: See de Bono's wonderful book, *The Six Thinking Hats*, rev. and updated (Boston: Little, Brown Book Group, 1999).

29   *It's akin to adopting:* Warren Berger, "What Zen Taught Silicon Valley (and Steve Jobs) About Innovation," *Fast Company*, April 9, 2012, www.fastcompany .com/1669387/what-zen-taught-silicon-valley-and-steve-jobs-about-innovation.

     A good question will be: Kevin Kelly, *The Inevitable: Understanding the 12 Technological Forces That Will Shape Our Future* (New York: Penguin Books, 2017), 288-89.

     If you ask questions: Keith Ferrazzi, *Never Eat Alone: And Other Secrets to Success, One Relationship at a Time* (New York: Currency Doubleday, 2005), 216.

     Do you want to sell: Zoe Chance, *Influence is Your Superpower: How to Get What You Want Without Compromising Who You Are* (New York: Random House, 2022), 100-101.

30   *Asked the same question repeatedly:* Scott Gilbey, "I Know Why Your Customer Service Sucks," *Entrepreneur US*, July/August 2024, 52-60.

     An effective brainstorming exercise: Taiichi Ohno, *Toyota Production System: Beyond Large-Scale Production* (Portland: Productivity Press, 1988), 29.

31   *Root of a difficult issue:* Eric Reis, "To Get to the Root of a Hard Problem, Just Ask 'Why?' Five Times," *Fast Company Magazine*, May 21, 2012, www .fastcompany.com/90186276/to-get-to-the-root-of-a-hard-problem-just -ask-why-five-times-2.

     A great teacher is: M. J. Aschner, "Asking Questions to Trigger Thinking," *NEA Journal* 50 (1961): 44.

     Enhancing learning among students: Dennis Palmer Wolf, "The Art of Questioning" (lecture, Summer Institute of College Boards of Educational Equality Project, Santa Cruz, CA, July 12, 1986).

     Every academic sector and field: Wolf, "The Art of Questioning."

32   *Money they could have earned:* Diana I. Tamir and Jason Mitchell, "Disclosing Information About the Self is Intrinsically Rewarding," *Proceedings of the National Academy of Sciences* 109, no. 21 (2012): 8038-43.

32   *Those who asked more questions:* Karen Huang et al., "It Doesn't Hurt to Ask:
      Question-Asking Increases Liking," *Journal of Personality and Social Psychology*
      113, no. 3 (2017): 430-52.

35   *Questions elicit answers in their likeness:* Krista Tippett, *Becoming Wise: An In-
      quiry into the Mystery and Art of Living* (New York: Penguin, 2016), 29.

36   *It's hard to resist:* Tippett, *Becoming Wise*, 29.
      The exploration of questions: Barbara Benedict, *Curiosity: A Cultural History of
      Early Modern Inquiry* (Chicago: University of Chicago Press, 2001), 1.
      Albert Einstein perceived curiosity: Brian Grazer and Charles Fishman, *A Cu-
      rious Mind: The Secret to a Bigger Life* (New York: Simon & Schuster, 2015), 17.
      An eager wish to learn: Cambridge Dictionary Online, s.v. "curiosity (*n.*)," www
      .dictionary.cambridge.org/dictionary/english/curiosity.

37   *I did not ask for:* Abraham Joshua Heschel, *God in Search of Man: A Philosophy
      of Judaism* (New York: Farrar, Straus and Giroux, 1955).
      What David Brooks calls an active curiosity: David Brooks, *How to Know a
      Person: The Art of Seeing Others Deeply and Being Deeply Seen* (New York:
      Random House, 2023), 33.
      Curiosity grows from: Liz Wiseman, *Rookie Smarts: Why Learning Beats
      Knowing in the New Game of Work* (New York: HarperCollins, 2014), 149.

38   *To be curious is:* Phone conversation with Heather Holleman, author of *The Six
      Conversations*, a book I highly recommend.
      I know more about: Warren Berger, *A More Beautiful Question: The Power of
      Inquiry to Spark Breakthrough Ideas* (New York: Bloomsbury, 2014), 16.
      The most fundamental question: Dyer, Gregersen, and Christensen, *The Innova-
      tor's DNA*, 77-78.
      We need to possess: Warren Berger, *The Book of Beautiful Questions: The Powerful
      Questions That Will Help You Decide, Create, Connect, and Lead* (New York:
      Bloomsbury, 2018), 4.

3. LIVING A QUESTION-ORIENTED LIFE

40   *On a warm summer Friday night:* Allison Klein, "A Gate-Crasher's Change of
      Heart," *Washington Post*, July 13, 2007, www.washingtonpost.com/wp-dyn
      /content/article/2007/07/12/AR2007071202356.html.

43   *Stupid and naive questions:* In her book *Rookie Smarts* (New York: Harper
      Business, 2014), Liz Wiseman differentiates naive questions from stupid ques-
      tions this way: "Naïve questions are natural, innocent, and unaffected. A naïve
      question has no preconceived assumptions or answers and cuts to the core of
      the issue. Stupid questions lack intelligence and common sense. . . . Asking

naïve questions refreshes and invigorates thinking. Asking stupid questions is simply annoying" (55-56).

45 *Ask questions and reciprocate vulnerability:* I first read of this cycle in Charles Duhigg's *Supercommunicators: How to Unlock the Secret Language of Connection* (New York: Random House, 2024). For a more robust explanation, see pages 93-95 of his book.

50 *The report revealed that:* Liz Mineo, "Good Genes Are Nice, but Joy Is Better," *Harvard Gazette*, April 11, 2017, www.news.harvard.edu/gazette/story /2017/04/over-nearly-80-years-harvard-study-has-been-showing-how-to-live -a-healthy-and-happy-life/.

More evidence of loneliness: You can read more about this fascinating ongoing study in Robert Waldinger and Marc Schulz's book *The Good Life: Lessons from the World's Longest Scientific Study of Happiness* (New York: Simon & Schuster, 2023).

Leprosy of the West: Kendall Palladino, "Mother Teresa Saw Loneliness as Leprosy of the West," *News-Times*, updated November 16, 2009, www .newstimes.com/news/article/Mother-Teresa-saw-loneliness-as-leprosy-of -the-250607.php.

Growing health issues created by: Jason Daley, "The U.K. Now Has a 'Minister for Loneliness.' Here's Why It Matters," *Smithsonian Magazine*, January 19, 2018, www .smithsonianmag.com/smart-news/minister-loneliness-appointed-united -kingdom-180967883/.

Japan named their own minister: Katie Warren, "Japan Has Appointed a 'Minister of Loneliness' After Seeing Suicide Rates in the Country Increase for the First Time in 11 Years," *Business Insider*, February 22, 2021, www.business insider.com/japan-minister-of-loneliness-suicides-rise-pandemic-2021-2.

Four thousand people died alone: Lydia S. Dugdale, *The Lost Art of Dying: Reviving Forgotten Wisdom* (New York: HarperOne, 2020), 51.

Commonplace to rent pretend companions: Chris Colin, "The Incredibly True Story of Renting a Friend in Tokyo," *Afar Magazine*, February 19, 2016, www .afar.com/magazine/the-incredibly-true-story-of-renting-a-friend-in-tokyo.

A public health crisis: See Vivek H. Murthy, MD, *Together: The Healing Power of Human Connection in a Sometimes Lonely World* (New York: Harper, 2020).

Members of Gen Z: Katie Baskerville, "Gen Z Are So Lonely They're Posting Friendship Applications on Facebook," *Vice,* February 7, 2024, www.vice.com /en/article/n7em9x/friendship-applications-gen-z-loneliness.

51 *Collective cry of loneliness:* Freya India, "Aren't You Lonely?: Friendship Has Become Another Joyless Thing to Do on a Screen," *After Babel* Substack newsletter, July 5, 2024, www.afterbabel.com/p/arent-you-lonely.

51   *Isolation and loneliness have contributed:* You can read more about this in my
      book *A Time to Heal: Offering Hope to a Wounded World in the Name of Jesus*
      (Oviedo, FL: Higher Life Publishing, 2021), 80-83.

      Thought, patience, and respect: Steve Ogne and Tim Roehl, *TransforMissional
      Coaching: Empowering Leaders in a Changing Ministry World (*Nashville: B&H
      Publishing, 2008), 134.

      Yet it's often misunderstood: Robert E. Logan and Sherilyn Carlton, *Coaching
      101: Discover the Power of Coaching* (St. Charles, IL: Churchsmart, 2003), 33.

      Listening not only respects: Logan and Carlton, *Coaching 101*, 127.

      Chinese symbol for listening: Warren Berger, *The Book of Beautiful Questions:
      The Powerful Questions That Will Help You Decide, Create, Connect, and Lead*
      (New York: Bloomsbury, 2018), 114.

      Being heard is so close: David W. Augsburger, *Caring Enough to Hear and Be
      Heard: How to Hear and How to Be Heard in Equal Communication* (Grand
      Rapids, MI: Baker, 1982), 89.

52   *When I left the dining room:* Dick Leonard, *The Great Rivalry: Gladstone and
      Disraeli* (London: I.B. Tauris, 2013), 202-3.

      The Attention-Interaction Project: Charles Derber, *The Pursuit of Attention:
      Power and Ego in Everyday Life* (New York: Oxford University Press,
      2000), 106.

53   *What David Brooks dubs conversation toppers:* David Brooks, *How to Know a
      Person: The Art of Seeing Others Deeply and Being Deeply Seen* (New York:
      Random House, 2023), 81.

      An attention-giving posture that attempts: Derber, *Pursuit of Attention*, 47.

      Notice the different responses: Kate Murphy, *You're Not Listening: What You're
      Missing and Why It Matters* (New York: Celadon, 2019), 136-39.

      You can make more friends: Dale Carnegie, *How to Win Friends and Influence
      People* (New York: Simon & Schuster, 1998), 52.

54   *Attention is the rarest:* Simone Weil, *Gravity and Grace* (New York: Routledge,
      2002), 115.

56   *Fruit of the Spirit:* Christine Herman, "Why We Argue Best with Our Mouths
      Shut," *Christianity Today*, May 26, 2017, www.christianitytoday.com/ct/2017
      /june/why-we-argue-best-with-our-mouths-shut.html.

4. THE QUESTIONS WE ASK

63   *The Big Three are:* John Mark Comer, *Live No Lies: Recognize and Resist the Three
      Enemies That Sabotage Your Peace* (Colorado Springs: Waterbrook, 2021), 64-65.

      What is most fascinating: David Brooks, *How to Know a Person: The Art of Seeing
      Others Deeply and Being Deeply Seen* (New York: Random House, 2023), 135.

63   *The desire to ask:* In his book *The Divine Conspiracy* (Grand Rapids, MI: Zondervan, 2010), Dallas Willard shares three additional significant questions: *Which life is the good life? Who is truly a good person? How are we to live in response?* (97-98).

One reason religion has survived: Rabbi Jonathan Sacks, "We Are What We Remember," Chabad.org, Chabad-Lubavitch Media Center, www.chabad.org /parshah/article_cdo/aid/3424152/jewish/We-Are-What-We-Remember.htm.

64   *Was his identity based on:* Dietrich Bonhoeffer, "Who Am I?" in *Letters and Papers from Prison* (New York: Macmillan, 1972), 459-60.

He who has a why: Friedrich Nietzsche, *Twilight of the Idols* (Leipzig: C. G. Naumann, 1889), 118.

65   *If patients are unable to answer:* A. J. Swoboda, *The Gift of Thorns* (Grand Rapids, MI: Zondervan, 2024), 28.

To put this in perspective: Ethan Kross, *Chatter: The Voice in Our Head, Why It Matters, and How to Harness It* (New York: Crown, 2021), xxii.

When the answer to: Mike Foster, *The Seven Primal Questions: Take Control of the Hidden Forces That Drive You* (n.p.: Five Dates Publishing, 2023), 37.

The Seven Primal Questions: Foster, *Seven Primal Questions*, 35.

66   *You won't be asking:* Gordon MacDonald, *A Resilient Life: You Can Move Ahead No Matter What* (Nashville: Thomas Nelson, 2009), 50-51.

67   *Hard-hitting reflection questions:* Gordon MacDonald, *Building Below the Water Line: Strengthening the Life of a Leader* (Peabody, MA: Hendrickson Publishers, 2011), 34-35.

69   *Questions from David Brooks:* Brooks, *How to Know a Person*.

70   *Center of their universe:* David Brooks, *The Road to Character* (New York: Random House, 2015), 6.

Step back to ask: Charles Duhigg, *Supercommunicators: How to Unlock the Secret Language of Connection* (New York: Random House, 2024), 32-33.

5. THE GOD WHO ASKS

73   *God does not pose:* Heather C. King, *Ask Me Anything, Lord: Opening Our Lives to God's Questions* (Grand Rapids, MI: Discovery House, 2013), 9.

God knows questions create: Trevor Hudson, *Questions God Asks Us* (Nashville: Upper Room Books, 2008), 12.

God wants all of creation: Hudson, *Questions God Asks Us*, 12.

74   *Translating from the original:* If you can speak another language, you know it's some-times difficult to find an exact word-for-word translation that travels seamlessly from one context to another. It's not quite as cut-and-dried as we might desire, as translations are filled with nuance and additional context. One translation may

include a question mark at the end of a verse, while another translation of the same verse will choose to use an exclamation point. For example, the New Revised Standard Version (NRSV) forms Numbers 24:23 into a question, whereas the King James Version (KJV) uses an exclamation point. The same holds true for Luke 8:25 and 1 Corinthians 6:4. Additionally, some New Testament questions are also quotes from the Old Testament, and punctuation is changed due to context. In John 4:27, two such questions are never asked. So different translations have different totals. The KJV includes about 3,298 questions—2,274 in the Old Testament and 1,024 in the New. While we may struggle to pin down an exact number of questions in our Bible, we can confidently say this: there are a *lot* of questions in there.

74   *Divine questions demand responses:* Hudson, *Questions God Asks Us*, 2-3.
      It's possible Adam was: Carolyn Williford and Craig Williford, *Questions from the God Who Needs No Answers* (New York: Random House, 2003), 9.

78   *Job experiences God's power:* Although sixty-six are counted, some sentences contain more than one question inside of each question noted; therefore, an exact count is difficult to determine.

6. THE QUESTIONS JESUS ASKS

80   *The human brain processes:* Leonard Sweet, *From Tablet to Table: Where Community Is Found and Identity Is Formed* (Colorado Springs: NavPress, 2014), 30.
      Reading stories creates: Annie Murphy Paul, "Your Brain on Fiction," *New York Times*, March 17, 2012, www.nytimes.com/2012/03/18/opinion/sunday/the-neuroscience-of-your-brain-on-fiction.html.

81   *Jesus' stories had a question:* Marcus J. Borg, *Jesus: Uncovering the Life, Teachings, and Relevance of a Religious Revolutionary* (San Francisco: Harper & Row, 2005), 152-53.

82   *Almost all of them rhetorical:* Reading in the New International Version, they are: Matthew 5:13; two in 5:46; two in 5:47; 6:25; 6:27; 6:28; 6:30; three in 6:31; 7:3; 7:4; 7:9; 7:10; and 7:16.

83   *Most of his questions:* The Synoptic Gospels, with some variance, remain fairly close. In Matthew's Gospel, Jesus' questions are conversational about 50 percent of the time while being conversational approximately two-thirds (67 percent) of the time in Mark and approximately one-third (32 percent) of the time in Luke. In John's Gospel, by contrast, a large majority (92 percent) of Jesus' questions are conversational in nature. The Gospel of John, which emphasizes the truth of Jesus, only records 8 percent of Jesus' questions in his formal teachings.
      The Gospel of John: Jo-Ann A. Brant, *Dialogue and Drama: Elements of Greek Tragedy in the Fourth Gospel* (Peabody, MA: Hendrickson, 2004), 194.

86   *To be Jewish is:* Edgar M. Bronfman, "To Be Jewish Is to Ask Questions," *Washington Post,* March 25, 2013, www.washingtonpost.com/national/on-faith/to -be-jewish-is-to-ask-questions/2013/03/25/5d4219bc-9548-11e2-bc8a -934ce979aa74_story.html.

Uncertainty and mystery amid: Rabbi Lord Jonathan Sacks, "The Necessity of Asking Questions," Orthodox Union, accessed July 22, 2019, www.ou.org /torah/parsha/rabbi-sacks-on-parsha/the_necessity_of_asking_questions/.

Debates sparked by questions: Martin B. Copenhaver, *Jesus Is the Question: The 307 Questions Jesus Asked and the 3 He Answered* (Nashville: Abingdon, 2014), xxiv.

Jesus was called rabbi: Tom Hughes, quoted in Don Everts and Doug Schaupp, *I Once Was Lost: What Postmodern Skeptics Taught Us About Their Path to Jesus* (Downers Grove, IL: InterVarsity Press, 2008), 54.

87   *One thousand questions found in:* In his book *Questions and Rhetoric in the Greek New Testament: An Essential Reference Resource for Exegesis* (Grand Rapids, MI: Zondervan, 2017), Douglas Estes writes that of all the books in the New Testament, the four Gospels, Acts, Romans, 1 and 2 Corinthians, Galatians, Hebrews, and James offer the largest number of questions. Others include Philippians (eighteen), Revelation (eight), James (four), and 2 Peter (four). 2 Timothy, Titus, Philemon, 2 John, 3 John, and Jude contain no questions.

The most common number cited: Many people who use this number refer to Martin Copenhaver's book *Jesus is the Question: The 307 Questions Jesus Asked and the 3 He Answered.*

Direct questions of Jesus: 105 questions in Matthew, 67 questions in Mark, 101 questions in Luke, and 51 questions in John.

Adding it all up: If you eliminate the repeated questions in the overlapping stories of the Synoptic Gospels in the New International Version, that makes 235 unique questions of Jesus. Add in the question to Saul, and you get a total of 236.

Some questions may be: Douglas Estes, phone interview with author, October 18, 2018.

88   *Forty times more likely:* Copenhaver, *Jesus is the Question,* 87.

More likely asked you a question: Conrad Gempf, *Jesus Asked: What He Wanted to Know* (Grand Rapids, MI: Zondervan, 2003), 20.

Some have claimed that: Copenhaver, *Jesus Is the Question,* xi-xii.

90   *Center of pagan worship:* Caesarea Philippi was also called Panias or Banias in honor of Pan, the god of everything.

91   *Different types of questions:* Herman Harrell Horne, *Teaching Techniques of Jesus: How Jesus Taught* (Grand Rapids, MI: Kregel, 1971), 48.

Have you not read: Matthew 12:3, 5; 19:4; 22:31; Mark 12:10, 26.

91 *His use of exaggeration:* Adam Hamilton, "Why Do You See the Speck in Your Neighbor's Eye," in *What Did Jesus Ask? Christian Leaders Reflect on His Questions of Faith*, edited by Elizabeth Dias (New York: TIME Books, 2015), 9.

92 *"How much more" technique:* See Matthew 6:26, 30; 7:11.

From the stronger argument: In Hebrew it was called *qal va-homer* (literally "light and heavy"), made famous by the renowned Jewish rabbi Hillel.

If these seemingly small things: Also see Matthew 6:25-28, 30; 7:11; 12:12; Luke 11:13; 12:24, 28.

What is it that I'm seeking: Other pointed questions in John's Gospel include, "What will you do?" (Jn 6:30); "Do you take offense at this?" (Jn 6:61 ESV); "Will you lay down your life for me?" (Jn 13:38 ESV); "Whom do you seek?" (Jn 18:4 ESV); "Is that your own idea . . . or did others talk to you about me?" (Jn 18:34); and "Do you love me?" (Jn 21:15-17).

7. THE QUESTIONS WE ASK GOD

94 *What comes into our minds:* A. W. Tozer, *The Knowledge of the Holy: The Attributes of God; Their Meaning in the Christian Life* (San Francisco: HarperOne, 2009), 1.

My friend Kelly: Kelly Yordy, email correspondence with the author.

95 *Master questioners in our world:* Warren Berger, *The Book of Beautiful Questions: The Powerful Questions That Will Help You Decide, Create, Connect, and Lead* (New York: Bloomsbury, 2018), 7.

I think there is frequently: John Locke, *Some Thoughts Concerning Education,* 7: 120 (Modern History Sourcebook, 1692), https://origin-rh.web.fordham .edu/Halsall/mod/1692locke-education.asp.

A roomful of children: I learned this question—and the challenge to ask children—from Lacy Finn Borgo's book *Faith Like a Child: Embracing Our Lives as Children of God* (Downers Grove, IL: InterVarsity Press, 2023), 9.

96 *Whenever you find tears:* Frederick Buechner, *A Crazy, Holy Grace: The Healing Power of Pain and Memory* (Grand Rapids, MI: Zondervan, 2017), 60.

99 *Praying that God would:* There are many requests like these in what are called the imprecatory psalms (see Psalms 55, 59, 69, 79, 109, and 137).

100 *It's uncomfortable and angsty:* If you want to press in further with lament, I recommend Terra McDaniel's *Hopeful Lament: Tending Our Grief Through Spiritual Practices* and Soong-Chan Rah's *Prophetic Lament: A Call for Justice in Troubled Times.*

Mourning takes practice: A line I first read in James K. A. Smith's book *You Are What You Love: The Spiritual Power of Habit* (Grand Rapids, MI: Brazos Press, 2016), 133.

100   *Need psalms of lament:* I wrote about this more in depth in my previous book,
      Fail: Finding Hope and Grace in the Midst of Ministry Failure (Downers Grove,
      IL: InterVarsity Press, 2014).
      I have not lost faith: Elie Wiesel, *Night* (New York: Hill and Wang, 2006).
      The midst of pain: The only stark exception to this structure in the psalms of
      lament is Psalm 88, which ends with no resolution. It ends with: "You have
      taken from me friend and neighbor—darkness is my closest friend" (18). Some
      scholars have called it the darkest and most depressing of all the psalms.

8. QUESTIONS AS INFLUENCE

105   *The number one difference:* Liz Wiseman, *Multipliers: How the Best Leaders
      Make Everyone Smarter* (San Francisco: Harper Business, 2014), 97.

106   *Sentenced to death by:* Terry J. Fadem, *The Art of Asking: Ask Better Questions,
      Get Better Answers* (Upper Saddle River, NJ: FT Press, 2008), 180.

107   *Contribution to Western thinking:* One day in the car, when I recounted this
      story to my fourteen-year-old son (who doesn't always appreciate my love for
      questions), he asked if I'd ever considered drinking hemlock too.
      His mother was a midwife: I. F. Stone, *The Trial of Socrates* (New York: Anchor
      Books, 1989), 118.
      An adjective describing someone: Merriam-Webster Online Dictionary, s.v. "ma-
      ieutic (*adj.*)," www.merriam-webster.com/dictionary/maieutic.
      My art of midwifery: Tom Kerns, "Socrates as Midwife" (Philosophy 101,
      lecture, North Seattle Community College, Seattle, WA, November 1,
      2018), www.philosophycourse.info/lecsite/lec-socmidwife.html.

108   *The midwife receives her:* Christiana Rice and Michael Frost, *To Alter Your
      World: Partnering with God to Rebirth Our Communities* (Downers Grove, IL:
      InterVarsity Press, 2017), 65-66.
      Faith leaders as spiritual midwives: William M. Easum and Thomas G. Bandy,
      Growing Spiritual Redwoods (Nashville: Abingdon, 1997), 184-203.
      If a midwife sought: Rice and Frost, *To Alter Your World*, 65.

110   *The late leadership and organizational expert:* Frances Hesselbein, Marshall
      Goldsmith, and Richard Beckhard, eds., *The Leader of the Future: New Visions,
      Strategies and Practices for the Next Era* (San Francisco: Jossey-Bass, 1997), 227.

111   *The presence of leaders who:* Justin A. Irving and Mark L. Strauss, *Leadership in
      Christian Perspective: Biblical Foundations and Contemporary Practices for
      Servant Leaders* (Grand Rapids, MI: Baker Academic, 2019), 40.

112   *This sounds quite similar:* For a great exploration of how to be an Illuminator,
      read Brooks's opinion piece "The Essential Skills for Being Human," *New York*

Times, October 19, 2023, www.nytimes.com/2023/10/19/opinion/social-skills
-connection.html.

112   *Leaders amplify others by:* Erwin Raphael McManus, *Mind Shift: It Doesn't Take
a Genius to Think Like One* (New York: Convergent, 2023), 22.
Make a big difference: Jennifer Garvey Berger, interviewed in Shane Parrish,
"The Mental Habits of Effective Leaders," October 16, 2018, in *The Knowledge
Project,* published by Farnam Street, podcast, 1:30:06, https://theknowledge
project.libsyn.com/the-mental-habits-of-effective-leaders.

9. QUESTION-ASKING AS FORMATION

113   *What don't you like:* Meghan Larissa Good, "The Best Question I've Ever Been
Asked," *Meghan Larissa Good* (blog), January 13, 2024, www.meghan
larissagood.com/2024/01/13/the-best-question-ive-ever-been-asked/.

114   *What kind of old man:* First read in Gordon MacDonald's book *Building Below
the Waterline: Strengthening the Life of a Leader* (Peabody, MA: Hendrickson
Publishers, 2011), 28.

115   *Shallow copers:* Larry Crabb, *Inside Out* (Colorado Springs, CO: NavPress,
1988), 31.
How do I look: Robert Hyatt, Ecclesia Network Training Event (presentation,
Church on the Mall, Plymouth Meeting, PA, October 20, 2017).
Troubled reflectors: Crabb, *Inside Out,* 35.
What do I need to do: Hyatt, Ecclesia Network Training Event.
This honest assessment creates: Crabb, *Inside Out,* 35.
What is God doing: Hyatt, Ecclesia Network Training Event.

116   *A. W. Tozer's Self-Examination Questions:* Adapted from A. W. Tozer, *That Incredible Christian* (Chicago: Moody), 115-18.

117   *Jesus knew what Bartimaeus needed:* To add another layer to the story here, if
Bartimaeus was healed, he would almost certainly have had to learn a trade, get
a job, and spend his days working hard rather than sit day after day begging on
the roadside. (Who gives alms to a perfectly healthy person?) What Bartimaeus
desired was worthwhile, but *Bartimaeus* was the one who needed to realize that
what Jesus could willingly provide would cost him something significant—and
that sacrifice would be felt every single day of his life.

119   *One of my favorite:* It can also be spelled *chavrusa.*

121   *And why would God:* In 1843, Danish philosopher and theologian Søren Kier-
kegaard wrote *Fear and Trembling,* a book exploring this story. It's a fascinating
look at the story that engages courageously with these questions and many others.
Every red question mark: And don't forget to locate the one red question mark
in the book of Acts.

122   *I noticed something I hadn't before:* Pilate's six questions in Matthew 27: "Don't
you hear the testimony they are bringing against you?" (v. 13); "Which one do
you want me to release to you: Jesus Barabbas, or Jesus who is called the
Messiah?" (v. 17); "Which of the two do you want me to release to you?" (v. 21);
"What shall I do, then, with Jesus who is called the Messiah?" (v. 22); "Why?
What crime has he committed?" (v. 23).

Mark records that Pilate asked: Pilate's questions in Mark 15: "Are you the king
of the Jews?" (v. 2); "Aren't you going to answer? See how many things they are
accusing you of" (v. 4); "Do you want me to release to you the king of the Jews?"
(v. 9); "What shall I do, then, with the one you call the king of the Jews?" (v. 12);
"Why? What crime has he committed?" (v. 14).

The fourth Gospel was written: John recorded thirteen different instances of "tag"
questions in his Gospel. John 4:29 NET: "Surely he can't be the Messiah, can he?"
[woman at the well]; 6:67 NET: "You don't want to go away too, do you?" [Jesus
to his disciples]; 7:31 NET: "Whenever the Christ comes, he won't perform more
miraculous signs than this man did, will he?" [many in the crowd]; 7:35 NET:
"He is not going to go to the Jewish people dispersed among the Greeks and teach
the Greeks, is he?" [Jewish leaders to each other]; 7:41 NET: "No, for the Christ
doesn't come from Galilee, does he?" [the crowd with differing opinions of Jesus];
7:47-48 NET: "You haven't been deceived too, have you? None of the members
of the ruling council or the Pharisees have believed in him, have they?" [Phar-
isees]; 7:51 NET: "Our law doesn't condemn a man unless it first hears from him
and learns what he is doing, does it?" [Nicodemus]; 8:53 NET: "You aren't greater
than our father Abraham who died, are you?" [Judeans to Jesus]; 9:40 NET: "We
are not blind too, are we?" [Pharisees to Jesus]; 10:21 NET: "These are not the
words of someone possessed by a demon. A demon cannot cause the blind to see,
can it?" [people arguing about who Jesus was]; 18:17 NET: "You're not one of
this man's disciples too, are you?" [slave girl to Peter]; 18:25 NET: "You aren't one
of his disciples too, are you?" [people standing in the courtyard to Peter]; 21:5
NET: "Children, you don't have any fish, do you?" [Jesus to his disciples].

10. PREPARING TO ASK BETTER QUESTIONS

130   *Next-level question:* Some questions adapted from examples found in Charles
Duhigg, *Supercommunicators: How to Unlock the Secret Language of Connection*
(New York: Random House, 2024).

132   *Asking yourself a few specific questions:* Duhigg, *Supercommunicators*, 216.

Notecards full of questions: I did hear a story recently of a guy who brought a
stack of notecards full of questions on a first date to make sure he asked his date

the right ones throughout the night. Cringey as that might sound, he's been married to her for over three decades, so I guess it worked out all right for them.

134   *I've reread his book:* Larry King and Bill Gilbert, *How to Talk to Anyone, Anytime, Anywhere: The Secrets of Good Communication* (New York: Crown, 1994).

135   *What question do you hope:* A fantastic question from Heather Holleman in her book *The Six Conversations: Pathways to Connecting in an Age of Isolation and Incivility* (Chicago: Moody, 2022).
      We often learn more: Lloyd Alexander, *The Book of Three: The Chronicles of Prydain* (New York: Holt, Rinehart and Winston, 1964), 13.

136   *Questions that have patiently waited:* David Whyte, "Sometimes," in *Everything Is Waiting for You: Poems* (Langley, WA: Many Rivers Press, 2003), 23.
      I've emailed my questions: If you have any questions for me, feel free to email me at jrbriggs@kairospartnerships.org.

11. ENGAGING WITH QUESTIONS

139   *The same five words:* Stanley L. Payne, *The Art of Asking Questions* (Princeton, NJ: Princeton University Press, 1955), 138.

140   *The point is to be aware:* Jeff Dyer, Hal Gregersen, and Clayton M. Christensen, *The Innovator's DNA: Mastering the Five Skills of Disruptive Innovators* (Boston: Harvard Business Review Press, 2019), 89.

141   *This bad habit is called* boomerasking: Alison Wood Brooks and Michael Yeomans, "Boomerasking: Answering Your Own Questions," *Journal of Experimental Psychology: General* 154, no. 3 (March 2025): 864-93, https://doi.org/10.1037/xge0001693.

144   *Former FBI hostage negotiator:* Chris Voss, *Never Split the Difference: Negotiating as if Your Life Depended on It* (London: Random House, 2016), 3.

148   *Groups should attempt to generate:* Dyer, Gregersen, and Christensen, *Innovator's DNA,* 87.
      One of their dominating questions: Dr. Tanita Maddox offers the five spiritual questions Gen Z asks: *Do all people matter to God? Can I trust you? Am I safe? What is true? Am I enough?* in "5 Questions Gen Z is Asking: A Doorway for Biblical Conversations," *Logos,* accessed November 8, 2024, www.logos.com /grow/five-questions-gen-z-is-asking/.

150   *What question would I ask:* Charles Duhigg, *Supercommunicators: How to Unlock the Secret Language of Connection* (New York: Random House, 2024), 162.

RESOURCE 2: QUESTIONS TO ASK OURSELVES

175   *Gordon MacDonald's questions:* Gordon MacDonald, *A Resilient Life: You Can Move Ahead No Matter What* (Nashville, TN: Thomas Nelson, 2004), 52-58.

ABOUT THE AUTHOR

J.R. BRIGGS (DMIN, MISSIO SEMINARY) is the founding director of Kairos Partnerships, an organization committed to equipping hungry leaders through coaching, consulting, and speaking. He serves a wide variety of leaders, including business owners, pastors, Blackhawk helicopter operators, church planters, executive directors, bishops, college presidents, Chick-fil-A operators, and NCAA Division 1 college coaches. Before starting Kairos Partnerships, he served for fifteen years in ministry in megachurches, church plants, and house church networks.

He also serves with the Ecclesia Network as the director of Leadership and Congregational Formation, as a national trainer for Fresh Expressions, and as a guest instructor for Friends University in the Master of Spiritual Formation and Leadership program. He speaks and teaches regularly at conferences, retreats, colleges, and seminaries around the country.

J.R. has written over fifty articles, both online and in print, and has written, cowritten, and contributed to fifteen books, including *The Sacred Overlap*, *Fail*, and *Eldership and the Mission of God*. He lives with his wife and two sons in the greater Philadelphia area.

www.jrbriggs.com

www.kairospartnerships.org

ALSO BY J.R. BRIGGS

BOOKS

The Sacred Overlap: Learning to Live Faithfully in the Space Between
Fail: Finding Hope and Grace in the Midst of Ministry Failure
A Time to Heal: Offering Hope to a Wounded World in the Name of Jesus
Eldership and the Mission of God: Equipping Teams for Faithful Church Leadership (with Bob Hyatt)
Ministry Mantras: Language for Cultivating Kingdom Culture (with Bob Hyatt)

CONTRIBUTIONS

The Message Remix: Solo
The Abide Bible
The Abide Bible Course Study Guide (with Phil Collins and Randy Frazee)
Wine in the Word Bible Study Guide (with Gisela H. Kreglinger and Randy Frazee)

Like this book?

Scan the code to discover more content like this!

Get on IVP's email list to receive special offers, exclusive book news, and thoughtful content from your favorite authors on topics you care about.

ivp | InterVarsity Press